THE 30-MINUTE KOSHER COOK

ALSO BY JUDY ZEIDLER

The Gourmet Jewish Cook

Judy Zeidler's International Deli Cookbook

Master Chefs Cook Kosher

COAUTHOR
Michel Richard's Home Cooking with a French Accent

THE 30-MINUTE KOSHER COOK

MORE THAN 130 QUICK AND EASY GOURMET RECIPES

＊

JUDY ZEIDLER

WILLIAM MORROW AND COMPANY, INC.

NEW YORK

It is the policy of William Morrow and Company, Inc., and its
imprints and affiliates, recognizing the importance of
preserving what has been written, to print the books we
publish on acid-free paper, and we exert our best
efforts to that end.

Library of Congress Cataloging-in-Publication Data

Zeidler, Judy.
The 30-minute kosher cook : more than 130 quick and easy gourmet
recipes / Judy Zeidler.
p.   cm.
Includes index.
ISBN 0-688-15533-2
1. Cookery, Jewish.   2. Kosher food.   3. Quick and easy cookery.
I. Title.
TX724.Z447   1999
641.5'676—dc21   98-27552
CIP

Printed in the United States of America

First Edition

1 2 3 4 5 6 7 8 9 10

BOOK DESIGN BY JO ANNE METSCH

www.williammorrow.com

TO MY HUSBAND,

*Marvin, the most creative 30-minute chef I know;
for contributing his original recipes to this book,
and most of all for his encouragement and support
and his on-target criticism*

ACKNOWLEDGMENTS

At William Morrow: Naomi Glickman, for her idea of a 30-minute kosher cookbook and for asking me to write it; Justin Schwartz and Christy Stabin, for continuing the job and getting this beautiful book out on schedule; Sonia Greenbaum, for her thorough copyediting.

My agent, Fred Hill, for his encouragement. Janice Wald Henderson for her excellent editing. Joan Bram, Carolee Blumin, and Sylvia Fox, my tireless testers.

A special thanks to my family: Marc, Leo, and Jay for keeping my software updated and getting me out of jams. Daughter Sue and two granddaughters Ariella and Melina, my testers and tasters in Portland. The rest of my children, Judy, Kathy, Steve, Paul, Amber, and Zeke, and grandchildren, Aaron, Normandie, Giamaica Day, Zane, and Quest, for their critique of these recipes at our family gatherings.

Sara J. Mitchell for her enduring friendship, and for always knowing what I wanted to say and helping me say it.

A SPECIAL note of thanks for the continued inspiration derived from the Brovelli family and the Santini family, our friends in Italy.

CONTENTS

INTRODUCTION

Our lives are whirlwinds. We rush to work, even car pool, we run to the cleaners and, if we're lucky, we work out at the gym. Most of us are also chauffeurs, ferrying our children to Little League, soccer games, piano lessons, and of course Hebrew school. And since so many families have two careers, who's going to cook dinner at the end of a long workday? Most important, we not only want to prepare home-cooked food, we want it to be nutritious and taste good too. I wrote this book keeping all of these things in mind. I would like *The 30-Minute Kosher Cook* to be a lifesaver for anyone who wants to make a delicious meal prepared from fresh ingredients in 30 minutes or less.

When my children were little, I relied on different ways of cooking dinner without a lot of fuss. For example, I'd throw a brisket and vegetables into the oven and let them bake together for hours. But those heavy meat-laden menus don't work for me anymore. Like most other Americans, I like to eat lighter meals based on fresh vegetables, grains, fish, and poultry. And I want to cook them quickly, so I turn to such cooking techniques as steaming, broiling, and grilling. Today, the only time I slow-roast meat or turkey is for Passover, Rosh Hashanah, and other Jewish holidays.

Over the years I've developed a lot of ideas on how to minimize time in the kitchen without sacrificing quality or taste. For starters, I keep my pantry, refrigerator, and freezer full of the basics, such as seasonings, vegetables, and stocks (see pages 2–4). This means I almost always have ingredients on hand to make a meal. Labor-saving equipment, like the electric mixer, ice cream maker, blender, and food processor save so much food prep time. Before you begin cooking from this book, read Chapter One, "Cooking by the Clock." It's chock-full of information on how to develop your own, superefficient kosher kitchen.

While I keep a well-stocked kitchen, some of my favorite dinners are based on what I find ripe and fresh at the supermarket, fish emporium, or farmers' market. I am always amazed at how creativity is stimulated by fabulous ingredients.

Although this book features kosher recipes, these dishes work for everyone who enjoys good fresh food, quickly prepared. And I've made sure to give each dish some style, for food should be visually tempting too.

If you've read my earlier book, *The Gourmet Jewish Cook*, you know that I have my own ideas on kosher cooking. My recipes don't focus exclusively on traditional Jewish food. I can take almost any dish—Mexican, French, Moroccan, or Asian—and adapt it to kosher dietary laws. Since my husband, Marvin, and I spend several months each year in Italy, cooking and sampling regional foods and wine, I have a particular interest in adapting Italian recipes, and you will notice a strong Italian influence throughout this book.

Whether you're cooking for family or friends, food preparation should be quick and easy as well as gratifying. And remember, anything you make is always going to taste better than any take-out. So take a peek into my kosher kitchen and see what works for yours. I promise you many marvelous meals that never skimp on quality, yet demand little of your very precious time.

CHAPTER ONE

✳

COOKING
BY THE CLOCK

YOUR book club wants to change its locale and meet at your house? That means at least six people are coming to dinner in four hours. It's too late to plan a menu or run to the supermarket and then start cooking. Ordering Chinese food or pizza is uncreative, not to mention unkosher. So I like to follow the Boy Scout motto, Be Prepared.

Your refrigerator, freezer, and pantry shelves should be stocked with basic items that will provide delicious, savvy meals for instant entertaining or last-minute family dinners.

For starters, never underestimate leftovers. Vegetables can be transformed into soups, salads, and sauces. A cooked chicken breast can be made into Chinese specialties, sandwiches, or curried chicken salad. Cooked seafood can magically reappear in a cocktail. Fruits and berries are naturals for sorbets, shortcakes, sundaes, fruit cocktails, and salads. Buzzed in a blender, they turn into a thick sauce.

My refrigerator and freezer are probably larger than most, and I have lots of shelf space, but I thought it might be fun to make an inventory of what I have on hand, so you can compare it with yours.

The following three sections contain suggestions to help you prepare for any emergency entertaining or last-minute family meals.

THE QUICK FIX PANTRY

Important Staples Always to Keep on Hand

Adapt this list to your own preferences, and make a shopping list that works for you:

almond extract
anchovies
anise extract
apricot preserves
baking powder
baking soda
balsamic vinegar
barley
black peppercorns
brown sugar
bulgur
canned pumpkin
canned tomatoes
canned tuna
capers
chocolate (semisweet)
cocoa
cornmeal
cornstarch
dried pasta
flour

honey
Karo syrup
lentils
maple syrup
matzah meal
molasses
olive oil
pareve powdered chicken stock
popcorn
quick-cooking cereals
quick-cooking grains
raisins
red wine vinegar
rice
salt
soy sauce
sugars
tomato paste
tomato sauce
vanilla beans
vegetable oil

Herbs and Spices

When cooking time is short, assertive herbs and spices can still deliver big taste:

allspice
basil
cinnamon
cumin
dill
dried mustard
fennel seeds
nutmeg

oregano
paprika
pickling spices
rosemary
sage
tarragon
thyme

A LOOK INTO MY REFRIGERATOR

Juices and Condiments

apple juice

catsup

horseradish

mayonnaise

mustard

nondairy creamer

peanut butter

preserves

soy sauce

Tabasco sauce

wine (dry white or red)

Worcestershire sauce

Dairy Section

butter (unsalted)

buttermilk

cheese

cottage cheese

cream (heavy)

milk

sour cream

yogurt (nonfat and low-fat)

Fresh Vegetables and Fruit

apples

avocados

bell peppers

broccoli

cabbage

carrots

cauliflower

cilantro

cucumbers

garlic

grapefruit

green onions

lemons

lettuce

mushrooms

onions

oranges

parsley

parsnips

squash

tomatoes

THE TIME-SAVER FREEZER

Depend on your freezer to save precious time. The freezer should be used not only to store uncooked packaged foods but also to hold cooked items, such as soups, stocks, baked goods, and prepared dough, and to keep family favorites on hand, like chocolate-chip ice cream, coffee cake, and quick breads.

The following is a great basic shopping list—items I depend upon for short cuts, including ideas I've borrowed from famous chefs. Remember, you don't have to cook from scratch to be a fabulous cook. (Store items in Tupperware by color: red for meat foods and blue for dairy foods—for meat menus or milk menus.)

Baked Goods

bagels
breads
cakes
cookie dough
rolls

Poultry and Meats

Uncooked ground beef and veal
Uncooked ground chicken and turkey
Uncooked whole chicken

Fish

(There is no reason to freeze fresh fish because it is always available. I freeze only leftover cooked fish.)

Miscellaneous

assorted nuts
ice cream
sauces
shredded unsweetened coconut
sorbets

stocks (chicken, vegetable, and fish)
unsalted butter
unsalted nondairy margarine

YOUR FOOD PROCESSOR AND BLENDER

There are so many ways your food processor or blender can help cut preparation time. Here are some of my favorite time-savers to use with the recipes in this cookbook:

To Chop Vegetables and Fruits

- To obtain even-sized pieces, turn the blender or processor on and off quickly using a pulsing technique.
- Use blender or processor to chop parsley quickly. Dry parsley with paper towels beforehand so you don't make a paste. One half cup stemmed parsley yields ¼ cup chopped or minced parsley.

To Make Bread and Cookie Crumbs

- For soft bread crumbs, tear pieces of bread, trimmed of crust, into quarters. Using pulsing technique, blend or process 3 or 4 slices at a time. One slice of bread makes ¾ cup of crumbs. Store in refrigerator or freezer. Use in recipes and as a quick casserole-topper.
- To make cookie crumbs for pie crusts, process cookies until they turn to crumbs: just add sugar and butter or margarine and press into pie pan.

To Chop or Grind Nuts

- Turn the processor or blender on and off quickly using a pulsing technique. If you want to grind the nuts into a flour for cakes, it is best to add some of the sugar or flour from the recipe to avoid turning nuts into a paste or butter.

General Uses for Your Food Processor

- Mixing ground meat with eggs and matzah meal for meat loaf
- Mixing ground fish for gefilte fish with other ingredients
- Grating Parmesan and other hard cheeses
- Pureeing vegetables for soups and sauces
- Blending large quantities of foods, such as cracker crumbs or raw vegetables, in several small batches so you can control the texture

TIPS FOR 30-MINUTE COOKING

- Always cook an extra portion of fresh vegetables, so it can be tossed into the next day's salad bowl with fresh greens.
- Collect all your recipes and read them over carefully before you begin to cook. Be sure to have all the ingredients at hand and measured before you begin cooking or baking. Do you have all the ingredients you need? Is all the equipment on hand? It's amazing how much valuable time can be lost by looking for a whisk or other necessary utensils.
- Learn to do several tasks at once. For example, while the pasta is boiling, wash and dry the salad greens. While the meat is browning, mix your vinaigrette or sauce.
- If the broiler, grill, or oven requires preheating, do it before beginning your food preparation.
- When cooking time is short, turn to assertive herbs, spices, and aromatics to deliver big taste.
- When adding stock, wine, or water to ingredients that are already simmering, bring the liquid to a boil first. (Note: It's quick and easy to do this in a microwave.) This cuts the overall cooking time, because the temperature of the other ingredients won't be lowered.
- For timesaving, easy cleanup when baking fish, chicken, or meat, always line the roasting pan with heavy-duty aluminum foil.
- Sharpen knives periodically; they'll perform faster for you.

CHAPTER TWO

✳

APPETIZERS
AND
FIRST COURSES

I N the United States, we use the word "appetizer" for hot or cold hors d'oeuvres. In Italy these tidbits are called *antipasti,* meaning "before the pasta," and are served as a start to the evening meal. Antipasti often consist of many varieties of salami, olives, and raw or cooked vegetables.

I love to serve appetizers. But to ensure that guests are never full before dinner, I don't serve too many. To me, appetizers are like icebreakers, and are capable of setting a festive mood. I often serve two or three (never more) small ones. They are meant to stimulate the appetite, not satiate it.

I usually serve appetizers in the living room as soon as guests arrive. I supply plenty of napkins or small plates if the appetizers require a knife and fork. Sometimes I serve these small tastes as first courses at the table—often the entire dinner is a bevy of "first courses" for a wonderful grazing-type meal.

In this chapter you'll find a variety of appetizers that range from simple to sophisticated. I've selected recipes that require the least time to prepare, making them perfect for impromptu entertaining.

For a modern Jewish starter, try the Cheese Kreplach enriched with goat cheese. Or experiment with Thomas Keller's upscale take on latkes. These delicate mashed potato pancakes are irresistibly light and topped with salmon caviar.

On my yearly visits to Italy, I am always inspired by the wonderful antipasti. Caponata and Bruschetta with Spinach and White Beans are two dishes I frequently prepare. And when I have the urge to go exotic, I make Garbanzo Bean Hummus with Mint—this lower-in-fat dip is made in minutes and goes well with fresh vegetables, toasted pita, or bagel chips.

APPETIZERS AND FIRST COURSES

Fennel "Caviar"

Garbanzo Bean Hummus with Mint

Quick Basic Pizza Dough

Tomato, Onion, Rosemary Focaccia

Broadway Deli Rosemary Cracker Bread

Grissini (Italian Breadsticks)

Cheese Kreplach

Warm Smoked Salmon Carpaccio

Grilled Stuffed Mushrooms

Caponata (Eggplant Relish)

Marvin's Paper-Thin Frittata

Jonathan Waxman's Red Pepper Pancakes with Salmon Caviar

Roasting Peppers

Bruschetta with Spinach and White Beans

Thomas Keller's Mashed Potato Latkes

Bagna Cauda alla Piemontese

Skewered Japanese Eggplant with Peanut Sauce

FENNEL "CAVIAR"

FORGET CHOPPED liver. Instead, serve this fresh fennel pâté with its unexpectedly delicate anise flavor. The recipe is courtesy Alain Ducasse's lovely bed-and-breakfast, La Bastide de Moustier, in Moustier, France. One of my tasters confessed that she ate the whole bowlful of this "caviar" herself—she didn't even stop to make the accompanying toast rounds.

MAKES 2 CUPS; OR ABOUT 16 SERVINGS

2 medium fennel bulbs
¼ cup extra-virgin olive oil
3 garlic cloves, minced
1 shallot, minced
2 tablespoons minced yellow onion
Pinch of fresh minced thyme
Salt and freshly ground black pepper to taste
Toasted rounds of French bread

Cut off the feathery tops of the fennel bulbs, and remove any tough outer layers. Cut the fennel into ¼-inch dice, to yield about 3 cups.

In a large nonstick skillet over medium heat, heat the olive oil and sauté the garlic, shallot, and onion about 4 minutes, or until soft. Add the fennel and sauté until tender, about 10 minutes. Add the thyme, salt, and pepper, and let cook for 5 more minutes. Transfer to a wooden board and chop until well blended, or place in a food processor and pulse once or twice for a finer consistency. Spoon into a covered bowl or crock and refrigerate until ready to serve. Serve with toast rounds.

GARBANZO BEAN HUMMUS WITH MINT

IN **MIDDLE** Eastern cooking, garbanzo beans are blended with tahini, garlic, fresh lemon juice, and olive oil to make hummus, a rich, aromatic sauce that can be drizzled over falafel.

In this version, I've omitted the olive oil and used cumin and cayenne to give the hummus a little zing. I also added lots of mint, the key flavor to this healthful dip. Serve with fresh vegetables, toasted pita bread, or bagel chips.

MAKES ABOUT 3½ CUPS

Two 15-ounce cans garbanzo beans, drained; reserve 1 cup liquid
4 scallions, chopped
½ cup fresh lemon juice
4 garlic cloves, peeled
1 teaspoon salt
½ teaspoon freshly ground black pepper
½ teaspoon cumin
¼ teaspoon cayenne pepper
1 tablespoon soy sauce
½ cup tahini (see Note)
8 parsley sprigs
10 mint leaves

In a blender or food processor fitted with the steel blade, puree the garbanzo beans, reserved liquid, and scallions. Add the lemon juice, garlic, salt, pepper, cumin, cayenne, soy sauce, tahini, parsley, and mint leaves, and process until smooth. Add additional salt and pepper to taste, if necessary. Cover with plastic wrap and chill until ready to serve.

NOTE: *Tahini (crushed sesame seeds) is available at natural food and Middle Eastern grocery stores and at most supermarkets.*

QUICK BASIC PIZZA DOUGH

IMAGINE A fresh-baked batch of pizza, cracker bread, focaccia, or breadsticks that you can prepare in 20 minutes using this one basic recipe. Here are a couple of suggestions for quick pizza toppings: cream cheese and smoked salmon or goat cheese and basil. My personal preference is lots and lots of cheese, melted to perfection. Or experiment with some fun topping ideas of your own.

MAKES 1 BATCH DOUGH

2 packages dry yeast
Pinch of sugar
1¼ cups warm water
¼ cup extra-virgin olive oil
3½ cups unbleached all-purpose flour
1 teaspoon salt

In a small bowl, combine the yeast, sugar, and ½ cup of the warm water. Set aside until yeast becomes frothy, 2 to 3 minutes.

In the large bowl of an electric mixer, or using a hand mixer, combine the remaining ¾ cup water, olive oil, and the yeast mixture. Add 1 cup of the flour and the salt, blending well. Add the remaining flour, 1 cup at a time, gradually blending until a rough ball forms.

Transfer to a floured board and knead until the top of the dough is smooth and elastic, and springs back when pressed with a finger. If using immediately, cover with a towel and tear off desired pieces of dough. Or place in a plastic bag, seal, and refrigerate; it will keep for up to 4 days.

TOMATO, ONION, ROSEMARY FOCACCIA

OUR DEAR friends Wolf and Bettina Rogosky served us this incredible pizza when we visited them in Italy.

It's faster to make than ordering pizza from takeout, and it tastes so much better. Use my basic dough, and you can make this fragrant focaccia in a half hour.

MAKES 4 FOCACCIA; OR 32 PIECES; ABOUT 16 SERVINGS

1 recipe Quick Basic Pizza Dough (page 11)
½ cup extra-virgin olive oil
½ cup cornmeal
8 medium tomatoes, thinly sliced
4 medium yellow onions, peeled and thinly sliced
½ cup fresh whole rosemary, stemmed
Salt and freshly ground black pepper to taste

Preheat the oven to 450°F.

Prepare the Quick Basic Pizza Dough. Divide into 4 parts. Brush four 12 × 14-inch baking sheets with oil and sprinkle with cornmeal. Roll out each piece of dough to 8 × 10 inches; place on the prepared baking sheet and gently push the dough with your fingertips, reaching as close to the edges of the baking sheet as possible without tearing the dough. On top of each focaccia, arrange the tomato slices in a single layer; top with the onion slices, and sprinkle with rosemary. Drizzle with olive oil, and then sprinkle with salt and pepper. Bake on the lowest rack of the oven for 20 minutes, or until golden brown. Cut into 3 × 4-inch pieces and serve immediately.

BROADWAY DELI ROSEMARY CRACKER BREAD

THESE MATZAHLIKE rounds are crisp, thin, and fragrant with fresh herbs. They're a big hit at our Broadway Deli, in Santa Monica, California.

MAKES 8 CRACKERS

½–1 cup coarsely chopped fresh rosemary
1 recipe Quick Basic Pizza Dough (page 11)
¾ cup extra-virgin olive oil
½ cup cornmeal
Salt to taste

Preheat the oven to 450°F.

Knead the rosemary into the Quick Basic Pizza Dough and divide the dough into 8 pieces. On a lightly floured board, knead and pat one of the pieces into a thin round. Using a rolling pin, roll the dough out to a 10- to 12-inch round (the thinner the better). Place on a lightly oiled and cornmeal-dusted 12-inch pizza pan or 10 × 14-inch baking sheet. Pierce the dough with the tines of a fork. Sprinkle with olive oil and salt. Bake on the lower rack of the oven for 10 minutes, or until golden brown. Repeat with the 7 remaining pieces of dough.

GRISSINI (ITALIAN BREADSTICKS)

I USE THE Quick Basic Pizza Dough to bake my favorite grissini. Instead of making long, thin breadsticks, you can form them into a variety of shapes—canes, pretzels, or even circles for party napkin rings.

MAKES ABOUT 4 DOZEN; OR ABOUT 12 SERVINGS

1 recipe Quick Basic Pizza Dough (page 11)
1 egg white, lightly beaten, for brushing
¼ cup kosher salt, for sprinkling
¼ cup sesame or poppy seeds, for sprinkling

Preheat the oven to 350°F.

For *hand-rolled breadsticks*: Divide the dough into 4 parts and roll out each portion on a floured board into a ½-inch-thick rectangle. Cut each rectangle into 2-inch squares (about 8 squares). Roll each square up tight (cigarette fashion) and then, back and forth under the palm of your hand, roll it into a long, narrow stick, as thin as a pencil, 10 to 12 inches long. Carefully transfer each stick to a foil-lined and greased baking sheet, placing them ¼ to ½ inch apart. Keep the sticks straight and pinch the ends down so they stick to the foil. Repeat until all the dough is used. Cover with a towel.

For *pasta machine breadsticks*: Pinch off a ball of dough 2 inches in diameter and flatten it with the palm of your hand to ½ inch thick. Lightly dust the dough with flour. Set the pasta machine rollers as far apart as possible. Guide the dough between the rollers and roll it through. Coat it with flour and feed the sheet through the wide noodle-cutting blades, cutting it into strips about ¼ inch wide and 10 to 15 inches long. Carefully transfer each stick to a foil-lined and greased baking sheet, placing them ¼ inch apart. Keep the sticks straight and pinch the ends down so they stick to the foil. Repeat until all the dough is used. Cover with a towel.

Let the breadsticks rise in a draft-free warm place, about 5 minutes, until round and puffy. Brush with the egg white and sprinkle with kosher salt and seeds. Bake for about 15 minutes, or until golden brown and crisp. Carefully transfer the breadsticks to wire racks and let cool.

CHEESE KREPLACH

LIKE **ITALIAN** calzone, these bite-size cheese kreplach are perfect for a dairy Rosh Hashanah dinner or Yom Kippur break-the-fast. Consider this recipe as just another creative way to use the time-saving, versatile Quick Basic Pizza Dough.

MAKES ABOUT 12, OR 6 SERVINGS

1 recipe Quick Basic Pizza Dough (page 11)
¼ cup extra-virgin olive oil
3 tablespoons cornmeal
2 cups mozzarella cheese, julienned
8 ounces goat cheese, crumbled
1 cup grated Parmesan cheese
1 tablespoon fresh oregano or basil, chopped, or 2 teaspoons dried oregano
Freshly ground black pepper to taste
1 egg, lightly beaten, for brushing

Prepare the Quick Basic Pizza Dough.

Preheat the oven to 450°F. Brush a 10 × 14-inch baking sheet with olive oil and sprinkle with cornmeal.

In a bowl, combine the three cheeses, oregano, and pepper, and mix well. Cover with plastic wrap and set aside.

Divide the dough into 4 pieces. Roll out each piece and cut into 4-inch rounds with a biscuit cutter or the rim of a glass. Place the cheese mixture on one half of each round. Drizzle with a few drops of olive oil. Brush the edges of the rounds with the beaten egg. Fold the dough over the filling to form a half-moon and press the edges of the dough firmly together. Bake for 15 minutes, or until golden brown.

WARM SMOKED SALMON CARPACCIO

THE BEST smoked salmon comes from Nova Scotia, Scotland, Norway, and Denmark. Elegant but easy, this variation of a classic dish makes a wonderful appetizer. Served warm, smoked salmon takes on a more subtle flavor. Serve with toasted pumpernickel or thin slices of challah.

MAKES 6 SERVINGS

¼ cup extra-virgin olive oil
12 slices smoked salmon
Freshly ground black pepper to taste
6 dill sprigs, for garnish

Preheat the oven to 375°F.

Place 6 ovenproof appetizer-size serving plates in the oven until the plates are very hot. Using pot holders, carefully remove the plates from the oven and spoon some olive oil in a thin layer in the center of each plate. Arrange 2 slices of smoked salmon on each plate; it will sizzle. Return the plates to the oven for 30 seconds, or until the salmon begins to turn slightly opaque. Remove from the oven, season with pepper to taste, and garnish with dill. Serve immediately.

GRILLED STUFFED MUSHROOMS

IN THE 1940s, stuffed mushrooms were wildly popular as an appetizer. Now with the dazzling array of mushrooms available on the market, this delectable tidbit is making a comeback. Portobello mushrooms are particularly flavorful (small ones are referred to as *cremini*), and can be purchased at farmers' markets and most supermarkets.

MAKES 4 SERVINGS

4 small (about 6 ounces) portobello mushrooms or 8 cremini or button mushrooms
3 garlic cloves, minced
Salt and freshly ground black pepper to taste
Extra-virgin olive oil
Toasted baguette slices

Separate the stems from the mushroom caps and mince the stems with the garlic. Season with salt and pepper. Brush a foil-lined 6 × 8-inch baking pan with olive oil. Place the caps on the pan and spoon the minced mixture into the caps. Drizzle olive oil on top. Heat the broiler to high. Broil the mushrooms for about 5 minutes, or until tender and the juices begin to run out.

Transfer the mushrooms to serving plates using a metal spatula. Serve with toasted baguette slices.

CAPONATA (EGGPLANT RELISH)

SERVED HOT or cold, this eggplant relish works as both an appetizer and a first course. One of the most common varieties of eggplant is the long slender Japanese eggplant, which ranges in color from lavender to purple. For a Sicilian touch, add a handful of raisins and toasted pine nuts.

MAKES 6 SERVINGS

¼ cup plus 2 tablespoons extra-virgin olive oil
6 unpeeled Japanese eggplant (about 1½ pounds), cut into ½-inch slices
1 small yellow onion, peeled and diced
2 garlic cloves, minced
1 medium green bell pepper, diced
¼ cup tomato sauce
¼ cup cold water
¼ cup balsamic vinegar
Salt and freshly ground black pepper to taste
Handful of raisins and toasted pine nuts, for garnish (optional)

In a large nonstick skillet over medium-high heat, heat ¼ cup of the olive oil and sauté the eggplant until it turns brown, about 5 minutes. Transfer to a plate and set aside. Add the remaining 2 tablespoons olive oil and sauté the onion, garlic, and green bell pepper until soft, about 5 minutes. Stir in the tomato sauce and water. Simmer until well blended, about 5 minutes. Return the eggplant to the skillet. Mix in the vinegar, salt, and pepper, and simmer over low heat until the eggplant is tender, about 10 minutes. Serve hot or cold, garnished with raisins and pine nuts.

MARVIN'S PAPER-THIN FRITTATA

WE ALWAYS have a couple of eggs in the refrigerator and some sage growing in our garden, which makes this recipe a perfect last-minute appetizer when friends unexpectedly stop by.

MAKES 4 SERVINGS

2 eggs, lightly beaten
¼ cup minced fresh sage
Salt and freshly ground black pepper to taste
2 tablespoons unsalted butter or unsalted nondairy margarine

In a medium bowl, beat the eggs and 2 tablespoons of the sage, salt, and pepper, and blend well. In a 10- or 12-inch nonstick skillet, heat the butter or margarine over low heat. Pour the egg mixture into the skillet, distributing it evenly. Cook until firm, about 3 minutes, lifting the outer edge to loosen it as it cooks. Carefully transfer the frittata to a large platter and cut into pie-shaped wedges. Sprinkle with the remaining sage and serve immediately.

JONATHAN WAXMAN'S RED PEPPER PANCAKES
WITH SALMON CAVIAR

JONATHAN **WAXMAN** is one California chef who took New York City by storm in the late 1980s. This was his signature appetizer when he opened Jams restaurant in the Big Apple. He shared the recipe with me, and years later I still enjoy serving it to company. This is a gourmet version of traditional latkes.

MAKES 8 SERVINGS

2 roasted red bell peppers (page 21)
½ cup fresh or frozen corn kernels
1 shallot, finely chopped
1 tablespoon extra-virgin olive oil
2 tablespoons unsalted butter
Salt and freshly ground black pepper to taste
1 cup heavy cream
1½ cups unbleached all-purpose flour
1 tablespoon baking powder
1 teaspoon salt
3 eggs, separated
Extra-virgin olive oil, for greasing skillet
2 ounces red salmon roe, for garnish
2 ounces chopped chives, for garnish
8 cilantro sprigs, for garnish

Chop one of the roasted peppers into ¼-inch dice. Cut the second pepper in half. Cut one half into very fine strips. Mince the other half, almost to the point of puree, and set aside.

Sauté the corn, diced pepper and pepper strips, and shallot in the olive oil and 1 tablespoon of the butter for 2 minutes. Season with salt and pepper, and add the cream. Simmer for 15 minutes over medium-low heat.

Sift the flour, baking powder, and teaspoon salt into a large bowl. Gently stir in the egg yolks until well mixed. In a separate, clean bowl, beat the egg whites to form soft peaks and fold them into the egg-yolk mixture. Fold in the reserved minced pepper mixture.

Grease a 10- or 12-inch skillet or griddle with olive oil. Cook 3-inch pancakes in the skillet over medium-high heat for 2 minutes each side, or until they turn golden brown. Keep warm.

Place the warm pepper-and-corn cream on each plate and top with 2 pancakes. Garnish with equal portions of the salmon roe, chives, and cilantro.

ROASTING PEPPERS

This technique for roasting and peeling peppers is easy to follow and foolproof. When roasted peppers are pureed in a food processor, they become a delicious sauce for Risotto Latkes (page 97) and many other dishes.

Preheat the oven to 375°F. Place a large sheet of foil over the lower rack of the oven. Place the whole peppers on the middle or top rack of the oven. Bake for 20 minutes, or until the skin has puffed and darkened slightly on top. Turn each pepper over and continue to bake for 10 to 15 minutes more. Remove from the oven, and while the peppers are still warm, very carefully peel off the skins, reserving the juices. Pull out the stems and discard the seeds. Cut the peppers into segments that follow their natural ridges. Use as directed in the recipe, or layer the peppers in a bowl with the reserved juices, adding enough olive oil to cover. Cover with plastic wrap and refrigerate up to 4 days.

BRUSCHETTA WITH SPINACH
AND WHITE BEANS

THIS is a specialty of Cinghiali Bianco, a restaurant in Florence. If Florence isn't on your itinerary, the next best thing is to prepare the bruschetta at home.

MAKES 4 SERVINGS

4 tablespoons extra-virgin olive oil

1 small onion, peeled and chopped

6 garlic cloves, minced (about 2 tablespoons)

½ teaspoon dried thyme

½ teaspoon dried sage

½ teaspoon crushed red pepper flakes

One 16-ounce can cannellini beans with liquid

Salt and freshly ground black pepper to taste

1 pound fresh spinach, washed, blanched (see Note), drained, squeezed dry, and finely chopped (⅛-inch pieces)

Juice of ½ lemon (about 2 tablespoons)

4 thick slices French or Italian bread

Heat 2 tablespoons of the olive oil in a medium saucepan over medium heat for 30 seconds. Sauté the onion until golden, about 3 minutes, add the garlic and cook 1 minute more. Add the thyme, sage, and pepper flakes. Stir a moment, then add the beans and their liquid. Simmer for 10 minutes, or until thick. Season with salt and pepper.

In a 10-inch nonstick skillet, heat 1 tablespoon of the olive oil, and sauté the spinach until heated through, about 5 minutes. Squeeze the lemon juice over it and transfer to a bowl to keep warm.

In an 8-inch nonstick skillet, heat the remaining tablespoon of olive oil and lightly brown the bread on both sides.

To serve, arrange the toasted bread on serving plates. Mound the beans on half of each slice of toast and the spinach on the other half.

NOTE: *To blanch the spinach, wash and stem the leaves. Place the wet spinach leaves in a heavy saucepan and steam over medium-high heat until wilted.*

THOMAS KELLER'S MASHED POTATO LATKES

THOMAS KELLER, chef-owner of the acclaimed French Laundry restaurant in Napa Valley, California, serves the lightest, most delicious mini-potato latkes topped with salmon roe. When I asked him for the recipe, he was gracious enough to share it.

MAKES ABOUT 3 DOZEN, OR ABOUT 8 SERVINGS

1½ pounds potatoes (3 medium), peeled
2 tablespoons unbleached all-purpose flour
2–3 tablespoons heavy cream, warmed slightly
2 eggs
Salt and freshly ground black pepper to taste
¼ cup vegetable oil, for frying
Salmon roe (see Note), for garnish

Cut the potatoes into 2-inch chunks. Place them in a saucepan with water to cover; bring to a boil. Reduce the heat and simmer about 15 minutes until easily pierced with a fork. Drain well. Push the potatoes through a ricer or fine sieve into a medium mixing bowl.

Stir in the flour and cream. Add the eggs and whisk until smooth. Season with salt and pepper.

In a large nonstick skillet over medium-high heat, heat 1 tablespoon of the oil. With a teaspoon, spoon the batter into the hot oil and flatten each spoonful with the back of the spoon to make small, thin latkes. Cook for about 2 minutes a side, turning only once, until lightly browned.

To serve, place 4 latkes on serving plates and top with salmon roe.

NOTE: *Salmon roe may be found in the deli section of most supermarkets, in gourmet shops, and kosher markets.*

BAGNA CAUDA ALLA PIEMONTESE

BAGNA CAUDA means "hot bath" in Italian; it's a delicious way to "bathe" both raw and steamed vegetables.

One time when we were in Italy, some friends invited us to dinner. The first course was pasta, and the main course was this classic Piemontese dish, usually served as an appetizer. One large platter was piled high with raw vegetables and another was filled with cooked vegetables. We each had our own special ceramic bowl with a candle at the bottom to heat the "bathing" liquid of fragrant anchovy sauce in which to dunk our vegetables.

MAKES ABOUT 1 CUP

1 whole head garlic, broken into cloves and peeled (about ¼ cup)
½ cup water
12 anchovy fillets, finely minced
½ cup extra-virgin olive oil
Salt and freshly ground black pepper to taste
Raw vegetables (fennel, carrots, celery, cucumbers, mushrooms, red radishes, Belgian
*   endive, red bell peppers)*
Steamed or grilled vegetables (artichokes, potatoes, asparagus, string beans)
1 large loaf country-style bread

In a small saucepan over high heat, cook the garlic and water, uncovered, for 10 minutes, or until the garlic is tender, and drain. Mash the garlic and anchovies with a fork or in a food processor to blend thoroughly. Add the olive oil in a thin stream. Season with salt and pepper. (The mixture may resemble separated mayonnaise.)

Transfer the anchovy sauce to a medium saucepan and simmer over low heat until hot, about 5 minutes. Pour into an earthenware fondue dish.

To serve, keep warm in a flameproof casserole or terra-cotta bagna cauda set. Dunk raw and cooked vegetables into the anchovy sauce, scooping up some of the sauce. Hold a piece of bread under the dipped vegetable so you don't dribble the sauce on the table. Eat the vegetable and then the bread.

SKEWERED JAPANESE EGGPLANT WITH PEANUT SAUCE

I WAS INSPIRED to create this recipe after a fabulous trip to Bali! Japanese eggplant is very small and tender and usually comes in a beautiful lavender shade, although you may find white- and purple-skinned varieties. If you don't have time to make the Peanut Sauce, a kosher version is available at some markets.

MAKES 4 SERVINGS

Peanut Sauce (recipe follows)
1 cup unbleached all-purpose flour
Salt and freshly ground black pepper to taste
4 Japanese eggplants, unpeeled and sliced ¾ inch thick
Extra-virgin olive oil, for sautéeing
Cilantro sprigs, for garnish

Prepare the Peanut Sauce; cover with plastic wrap and refrigerate.

In a shallow medium bowl, mix the flour with the salt and pepper. Dip the eggplant slices on both sides in the flour and shake to remove excess. In a medium nonstick skillet over medium-high heat, heat the olive oil and brown the eggplant rounds on both sides 2 to 3 minutes, or until tender. Thread 2 or 3 eggplant slices through wooden skewers, lollipop fashion. Arrange on a large platter, garnish with cilantro, and serve with Peanut Sauce.

continued

PEANUT SAUCE

2 tablespoons minced yellow onion
1 garlic clove, minced
1 stalk fresh lemongrass, white stem only, minced (optional)
1 tablespoon light brown sugar
1 teaspoon ground coriander
½ teaspoon crushed red pepper flakes
⅛ teaspoon cayenne pepper
½ cup Vegetable Stock (page 30)
½ cup chunky peanut butter
1 cup unsweetened coconut milk
Salt and freshly ground black pepper to taste

In a small saucepan, combine the onion, garlic, lemongrass (if using), brown sugar, coriander, pepper flakes, cayenne pepper, vegetable stock, peanut butter, coconut milk, and salt and pepper. Bring to a boil over medium heat, stirring until smooth; reduce the heat and let the sauce simmer 4 minutes. Remove from the heat and pour into a medium serving bowl. Cool and cover with plastic wrap; refrigerate up to 4 hours. Bring to room temperature before serving. Add additional vegetable stock if needed to thin the sauce.

CHAPTER THREE

✳

SOUPS AND STOCKS— THE BUSY COOK'S TIME-SAVER

SOUP is the original comfort food—it draws family and friends into the kitchen and soothes the weary soul after a long day at work. In the winter, the inviting aroma of simmering soup warms the home. In the summer, a chilled soup is an instant refresher.

Today's busy cooks often turn to high-sodium canned or packaged instant soups, but the taste—and nutrients—just aren't there. These soups may save time, but they rarely save money. Dollar for dollar, homemade soup costs much less to prepare and tastes, well, like real soup.

Soup is incredibly easy to make. Whenever you have a few minutes to spare, pull out a large pot and toss in whatever vegetables you have on hand. Celery, carrots, onions, tomatoes, parsnips, leeks, and fresh herbs simmered in water or stock until soft and full-flavored make a simple but delicious soup.

Any of the soups in this book need only a crisp green salad and some crusty bread to make a complete meal. Some, like Cold Cucumber and Spinach and Cold Tomato with Mozzarella, are refreshing and light. Others, like Lentil Soup, strike a heartier note. Romaine Lettuce Soup embodies all the best elements of a great salad, and Cream of Asparagus Soup possesses a particularly bright asparagus flavor, thanks to the use of the stalks as well as the tips.

To make the very best soups quickly, first prepare some stocks to store in the freezer. The basic stock recipes in this chapter should speed you along the path of preparation. If you don't have time to make stock, purchase storebought varieties only after reading the labels carefully to make sure they're low in sodium, preservative-free, and low-fat or fat-free.

Remember that soups freeze very well, so make enough to save for the proverbial rainy day. There's nothing like a bowl of piping-hot soup to come home to—especially if it was made weeks before and all you have to do is heat it up.

SOUPS AND STOCKS

STOCKS

VEGETABLE STOCK

FISH STOCK

CHICKEN STOCK

PAREVE CHICKEN STOCK

ROMAINE LETTUCE SOUP

LEEK AND POTATO SOUP

CAULIFLOWER SOUP

EGGPLANT SOUP

COLD CUCUMBER AND SPINACH SOUP

COLD TOMATO SOUP WITH MOZZARELLA CHEESE

BEET AND CARROT BORSCHT

MEATLESS CABBAGE BORSCHT

LENTIL SOUP

CREAM OF ASPARAGUS SOUP

Most of the recipes in this book rely on three basic stocks. Making stock is not complicated. In fact, the easiest stock needs no recipe: Just boil vegetables in water until reduced by half, then add salt and pepper. Store in the freezer in ice-cube trays, for easy defrosting later.

If you have vegetable, chicken, or fish stock in the freezer, here are a few suggestions to produce a delicious soup in less than 30 minutes:

- Vegetable stock—add any mixture of fresh vegetables, a rouille (see Note), or pesto sauce.
- Fish stock—add assorted fish, cooked potatoes, and pureed red bell peppers or fresh fennel.
- Chicken stock—add ground-chicken meat balls or poached chicken breasts, and/or kreplach and egg noodles.
- Garnishes—for eye appeal and added flavor, garnish with lemon slices, croutons, mint sprigs, diced tomatoes, cucumber, zucchini, grated cheese, sour cream, or a drizzle of olive oil.

NOTE: *Rouille is a garlicky sauce from Provence, similar to a spicy mayonnaise, and usually served with fish soup. I like to use this piquant sauce in a variety of dishes.*

VEGETABLE STOCK

¼ cup extra-virgin olive oil

4 medium yellow onions, peeled and chopped

5 carrots, peeled and chopped into ⅛-inch dice

1 parsnip, peeled and chopped into ⅛-inch dice

4 celery stalks, chopped into ⅛-inch dice

3 leeks, white and green parts, cleaned and chopped into ⅛-inch dice

3 bay leaves

4 garlic cloves, crushed

6 fresh thyme sprigs or 2 teaspoons dried thyme

½ cup chopped fresh parsley

8 peppercorns

Salt to taste

2 tablespoons soy sauce (optional)

Heat the oil in a large stockpot over medium heat and sauté the onions, carrots, parsnip, celery, and leeks until soft and lightly browned, about 5 minutes. Stir in the bay leaves, garlic, thyme, parsley, peppercorns, salt, and soy sauce, if using. Add 12 cups cold water and bring to a boil. Reduce the heat and simmer, partially covered, for 2 hours.

Season with salt to taste. Remove from the heat, strain, pressing as much liquid as possible from the vegetables, then discard them. Let the stock cool, about 15 minutes. Pour into containers, cover, and refrigerate or freeze until needed.

NOTE: *The vegetable stock can be stored in an airtight container, in the refrigerator 2 to 3 days, or in the freezer for up to 2 months. Heat stock to boiling before using.*

FISH STOCK

YOU CAN usually get fish bones at your local fish market. Be sure to remove the gills if you use fish heads, as they are often bitter.

MAKES ABOUT 1 QUART

3 tablespoons extra-virgin olive oil
2 medium yellow onions, peeled and cut into ¼-inch dice
3 garlic cloves, minced
3 medium carrots, peeled and cut into ¼-inch dice
2 celery stalks with leaves
10 fresh parsley sprigs
2 bay leaves
10 peppercorns
3 pounds fish (bones and heads), thoroughly rinsed

In a large stockpot over medium heat, heat the oil and sauté the onions, garlic, carrots, and celery until soft, but not browned, 3 to 4 minutes. Place the parsley, bay leaves, and peppercorns in a cheesecloth and tie securely with string. Add to the stockpot along with the fish bones with enough water to cover the bones by 2 inches, and bring to a boil. Reduce the heat and simmer, uncovered, for 25 minutes. Remove any scum that rises to the surface. Strain and discard the solids.

Refrigerate the stock for about 15 minutes and remove the fat from the surface and then refrigerate or freeze.

NOTE: *The fish stock can be stored, in an airtight container, in the refrigerator 2 to 3 days, or in the freezer for up to 2 months. Heat stock to boiling before using.*

CHICKEN STOCK

FOR A richer stock, place the chicken in a baking pan and bake at 400°F until golden brown, about 10 minutes, before adding it to the stockpot.

MAKES ABOUT 1 QUART

2 quarts cold water

2 pounds chicken necks, backs, and wings

2 carrots, peeled, trimmed, and halved

1 celery stalk, thinly sliced

1 medium yellow onion, peeled and thinly sliced

1 parsley sprig, 1 bay leaf, ¼ teaspoon dried thyme, and 3 peppercorns, tied in a cheesecloth

In a large stockpot over high heat, add the water, chicken, carrots, celery, onion, and herbs, and bring to a boil. Reduce the heat and simmer, partially covered, 3 to 4 hours, adding more water if needed to keep the ingredients immersed. Strain, let cool about 15 minutes, and remove the fat that has formed on top of the stock.

NOTE: *Can be stored, in an airtight container, in the refrigerator 2 to 3 days, or in the freezer for up to 2 months. Heat stock to boiling before using.*

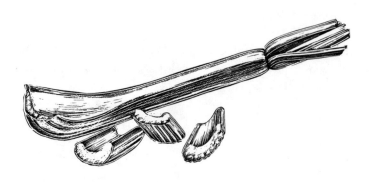

PAREVE CHICKEN STOCK

Pareve chicken stock is a commercial, powdered, chicken-flavored soup base that contains no chicken, meat, or dairy products. It may be used in all recipes for both dairy and meat meals. You can find it in most supermarkets in the kosher food department or in kosher markets. To reconstitute the stock, dissolve 1 tablespoon of the powder in 1 cup of hot water. Pareve beef stock is also available.

You can substitute pareve chicken stock for any recipe that calls for vegetable stock if you don't have any on hand.

ROMAINE LETTUCE SOUP

IF YOU'VE never tasted this salad favorite in a soup, you'll be surprised what a fresh and robust flavor romaine lettuce can impart.

MAKES 6 SERVINGS

2 tablespoons extra-virgin olive oil
¼ cup thinly sliced garlic, about 6 cloves
1 leek, cleaned and thinly sliced (white part only)
1 medium yellow onion, peeled and thinly sliced
2 celery stalks, thinly sliced
2 carrots, peeled and thinly sliced
1 parsnip, peeled and thinly sliced
4 cups Vegetable Stock (page 30)
3 cups chopped romaine lettuce (¼-inch pieces)
Salt and freshly ground black pepper to taste
Finely minced romaine, for garnish

In a large saucepan over medium heat, heat the oil and sauté the garlic, leek, onion, celery, carrots, and parsnip. Cook until tender, stirring occasionally, about 10 minutes. Add the stock, bring to a boil, cover, reduce the heat, and simmer until the vegetables are soft, about 15 minutes. In a food processor or blender, puree the mixture in 2 or 3 batches until smooth. Return the puree to the saucepan and add the romaine lettuce. Add the salt and pepper, and simmer for 5 minutes. To serve, ladle the soup into heated soup bowls. Garnish with finely minced romaine.

NOTE: *This soup can be stored, tightly covered, in the refrigerator 2 to 3 days, or in the freezer for up to 2 months. Defrost and heat before serving.*

LEEK AND POTATO SOUP

THE CLASSIC pairing of leeks and potatoes makes a delicious low-fat soup that tastes creamy even though it contains no cream. This soup is great to make when time is short, since the vegetables can be grated and chopped in the food processor. To give it more body, puree some of the vegetables in the food processor after they are cooked.

Double the recipe and freeze half for a day when you're too busy to cook.

MAKES 8 SERVINGS

3 garlic cloves, minced
1 medium yellow onion, peeled and chopped into ¼-inch dice
4 medium leeks, white and tender green leaves, cleaned and trimmed
3 tablespoons extra-virgin olive oil
1 large carrot, peeled and grated
2 large Idaho potatoes, peeled and thinly sliced (about 2 cups)
7 cups Vegetable Stock (page 30) or cold water
Salt and freshly ground black pepper to taste
1 cup grated Parmesan cheese, for sprinkling

In a food processor fitted with the steel blade or on a wooden board using a sharp knife, chop the garlic, onion, and leeks.

In a large saucepan, heat the olive oil and sauté the garlic mixture with the carrot and potatoes until soft, about 5 minutes. Add the stock and bring to a boil. Reduce the heat and gently boil, partially covered (this allows steam to escape, creating a good thick concentrated soup rather than one that's watered down) until the vegetables are tender, about 20 minutes.

The soup can be served at this point or, for a thicker smoother soup, remove from the heat, ladle 2 cups into a food processor, and blend until smooth. Return the pureed soup to the saucepan and season with salt and pepper. Bring to a simmer.

To serve, ladle the soup into shallow bowls. Sprinkle with Parmesan cheese.

NOTE: *This soup can be stored, tightly covered, in the refrigerator 2 to 3 days, or in the freezer for up to 2 months. Defrost and heat before serving.*

CAULIFLOWER SOUP

I USE THE core of the cauliflower as well as the florets in this recipe; just be sure to slice the core very thin. Salt and pepper are crucial to the success of this soup, so don't forget to add them—this soup is best when it tastes a little peppery.

We often serve glasses of sherry with this course and suggest that our guests pour a little into their soup.

MAKES 8 SERVINGS

2 tablespoons extra-virgin olive oil
1 medium leek or yellow onion, peeled, quartered, and thinly sliced
2 garlic cloves, minced
1 celery stalk, thinly sliced
2 carrots, peeled and thinly sliced
1 parsnip, peeled and thinly sliced
1 large cauliflower (1½ pounds), chopped (reserve a handful of florets)
5 cups boiling water
Salt and freshly ground black pepper to taste
Fresh dill sprigs, for garnish

In a large saucepan over medium heat, heat the olive oil and sauté the leek, garlic, celery, carrots, and parsnip for 5 minutes, stirring constantly with a spoon to avoid browning. Add the cauliflower and sauté 5 minutes more. Add the boiling water, return to a boil. Cover and lightly simmer for 15 minutes, or until the cauliflower is tender. Meanwhile, parboil the reserved florets in boiling water for 5 minutes, keeping them crunchy. Let them cool.

The soup is ready to serve at this point or, for a smoother, creamier texture, place the cauliflower mixture (with a little of the liquid) in a food processor or blender and puree in small batches. Return to the saucepan and simmer, mixing well. Season with salt and pepper.

To serve, ladle into shallow heated soup bowls and garnish with the reserved whole florets and sprigs of dill.

NOTE: *This soup can be stored, tightly covered, in the refrigerator 2 to 3 days, or in the freezer for up to 2 months. Defrost and heat before serving.*

EGGPLANT SOUP

I PREPARED THIS soup for one of my cooking classes, and months later a student called to tell me that she was heartbroken because she had lost the recipe. I found it and here it is! As good as this soup tastes when freshly made, the flavor is even better when reheated.

MAKES 6 SERVINGS

1 eggplant (about 1 pound)
3 tablespoons extra-virgin olive oil
1 yellow onion, peeled and thinly sliced
6 garlic cloves, minced
2 roasted red bell peppers (page 21), minced
Pinch of dried chili peppers (optional)
4 medium tomatoes, coarsely chopped
1 quart Vegetable Stock (page 30)
Salt and freshly ground black pepper to taste
Sour cream or yogurt, for garnish

Preheat the oven to 350°F.

Cut the eggplant in half lengthwise, brush with oil; place, cut side down, on a foil-lined baking sheet and bake until soft, about 15 minutes. Peel off the skin and discard. Cut the eggplant in cubes.

In a large saucepan over medium heat, heat the oil. Add the onion and garlic, and sauté until soft, about 3 minutes. Add the eggplant, bell peppers, dried peppers (if using), tomatoes, stock, and salt and pepper. Bring to a boil and simmer, partially covered, about 20 minutes.

The soup can be served at this point. Or remove from the heat; transfer it to a food processor or blender, and puree. Season with salt and pepper. Garnish with sour cream or yogurt.

NOTE: *This soup can be stored, in an airtight container, in the refrigerator 2 to 3 days, or in the freezer for up to 2 months. Defrost and heat before serving.*

COLD CUCUMBER AND SPINACH SOUP

THIS CREAMY, bright green soup even *looks* cool. It makes a great summer treat for dinner on the patio—or for lunch around the swimming pool, if you're lucky.

MAKES 8 SERVINGS

2 tablespoons unsalted butter or margarine

1 bunch scallions, thinly sliced

4 cups peeled and diced cucumbers (about 2 large)

3 cups Vegetable Stock (page 30)

1 cup chopped spinach

1 small potato, peeled and thinly sliced crosswise

½ teaspoon salt

Freshly ground black pepper to taste

Fresh lemon juice to taste

1 cup buttermilk

½ cup thinly sliced cucumber, for garnish

½ cup thinly sliced radish, for garnish

½ cup thinly sliced scallions, for garnish

In a saucepan, melt the butter and sauté the scallions until soft, about 2 minutes. Add the cucumbers, stock, spinach, potato, salt, and pepper. Simmer, partially covered, until the potato is tender, about 10 minutes. Add the lemon juice. Transfer the mixture to a food processor or blender and puree. Transfer to a bowl and stir in the buttermilk.

Let the soup cool, then chill it in the refrigerator for about 2 hours. Serve in chilled bowls, garnished with cucumber, radish, and scallions.

NOTE: *The soup can be stored, in an airtight container, in the refrigerator for 2 to 3 days.*

COLD TOMATO SOUP WITH
MOZZARELLA CHEESE

THIS IS Marvin's recipe, based on the famous Italian Caprese salad made with tomatoes, mozzarella cheese, and basil. It's fresh, colorful, and easy to prepare.

Another way to transform this recipe is to puree yellow tomatoes and spoon them over diced cucumbers and cubed squash. Sprinkle fresh julienned arugula over the top as a garnish.

MAKES 6 SERVINGS

6 medium tomatoes, peeled, seeded, and pureed (about 3 cups)
2 tablespoons sugar or to taste
½ teaspoon balsamic vinegar
1 teaspoon salt or more to taste
Freshly ground black pepper to taste
2 tablespoons minced fresh basil leaves
6 ounces soft mozzarella cheese, cut into 1-inch cubes
½ cup peeled and diced cucumber (½ small cucumber)
½ cup fresh corn kernels
Extra-virgin olive oil, for garnish

Strain the pureed tomatoes into a glass bowl. Add the sugar, balsamic vinegar, salt, and pepper. Add the basil and mix thoroughly. Spoon an equal amount of mozzarella, cucumbers, and corn kernels into the center of 6 shallow bowls and ladle some tomato mixture over each. Drizzle with olive oil, and serve.

In Italy, where cooks make tomato sauce all the time, we discovered a tomato press. It discards the seeds and skins, leaving a fresh tomato puree. This handy Italian-made device is made of heavy red acrylic, with a stainless steel strainer, and strong suction cup for attaching to any work surface. In Italy it can be found at any outdoor market or *casalinga* (kitchen-hardware store). In the United States you can find it at cookware stores priced at about $30.

BEET AND CARROT BORSCHT

BEETS AND carrots are both members of the root-vegetable family and taste most harmonious in this rich soup. Fresh ginger offsets the sweetness, and the sour cream garnish adds a mellowness with a little tang.

MAKES 4 TO 6 SERVINGS

1 quart cold water
½ pound (2 large) carrots, peeled and thinly sliced
½ pound baby beets, peeled and shredded
1 medium yellow onion, peeled and quartered
2 nickel-size pieces fresh ginger, peeled
Salt and freshly ground black pepper to taste
½ cup sour cream, for garnish

Bring the water to a boil in a 2½-quart pot. Add the carrots, beets, onion, and ginger. The water should just cover the beets. Cover, lower the heat, and simmer until the beets are soft when pierced with a fork, about 10 minutes.

Using a slotted spoon, transfer the vegetables and ginger to a food processor or blender, and puree until smooth, scraping the side of the bowl as necessary. Add the pureed vegetables to the liquid and stir until smooth. Add salt and pepper. To serve, ladle into heated soup bowls and garnish with sour cream.

NOTE: *This soup can be stored, in an airtight container, in the refrigerator 2 to 3 days, or in the freezer for up to 2 months. Defrost and heat before serving.*

MEATLESS CABBAGE BORSCHT

THIS IS a quick and easy version of a traditional sweet-and-sour cabbage soup. It takes only a few minutes to assemble; then let it simmer and forget about it for 25 minutes. This is great soup to have on hand in the freezer for unexpected company or when you don't have time to make dinner.

MAKES 6 SERVINGS

1 tablespoon unsalted butter or nondairy margarine
1 medium yellow onion, peeled and finely chopped
1 tablespoon minced garlic
8 cups Vegetable Stock (page 30)
1 large tomato, finely chopped
One 12-ounce can tomato sauce
½ cup sugar
½ cup white or cider vinegar
2 small heads green cabbage (3 pounds), shredded
Salt and freshly ground black pepper to taste
Fresh lemon juice to taste
1 cup sour cream, for garnish
6 fresh dill sprigs, for garnish

In a large saucepan, heat the butter or margarine over medium-high heat and sauté the onion and garlic until transparent. Add the stock, tomato, tomato sauce, sugar, vinegar, and cabbage. Bring to a boil partially covered and cook gently for 15 minutes; reduce the heat to low and simmer for 10 minutes. Add the salt, pepper, and lemon juice. Stir and simmer until heated through.

To serve, ladle into heated soup bowls and garnish with sour cream and dill.

NOTE: *This soup can be stored, in an airtight container, in the refrigerator 2 to 3 days, or in the freezer for up to 2 months. Defrost and heat before serving.*

LENTIL SOUP

ONCE YOU'VE made this delicately flavored soup, it will become a favorite. Serve with lemon wedges and squeeze a little juice into the soup when served. To save time, start making the soup while the lentils are soaking.

MAKES 8 SERVINGS

2 tablespoons extra-virgin olive oil

1 large yellow onion, peeled and diced

2 garlic cloves, minced

4 medium carrots, peeled and diced

1 medium parsnip, peeled and diced

2 celery stalks, diced

1 bay leaf

2 tablespoons minced fresh parsley

7 cups boiling water

1 cup lentils, soaked in cold water for 20 minutes and drained

1 teaspoon ground cumin

Salt and freshly ground black pepper to taste

½ cup Parmesan cheese, for garnish (optional)

Extra-virgin olive oil, for garnish

In a large stockpot over medium heat, heat the oil and sauté the onion, garlic, carrots, parsnip, celery, bay leaf, and parsley until soft, about 5 minutes, mixing with a wooden spoon to avoid sticking. Add the water; bring to a boil and add the drained lentils, cumin, salt, and pepper. Reduce the heat to medium, cover, and gently boil until the lentils are tender, about 25 minutes. Add additional salt and pepper to taste. Serve with Parmesan cheese, if using, or drizzle with olive oil.

NOTE: *This soup can be stored, in an airtight container, in the refrigerator 2 to 3 days, or in the freezer for up to 2 months. Defrost and heat before serving.*

CREAM OF ASPARAGUS SOUP

I NEVER DISCARD asparagus stalks; the more stalks, the better-tasting the soup. One night when we served asparagus tips as a salad with poached eggs, we saved the stalks to make a rich, creamy soup that lasted for 4 days. Each day we transformed the soup with a different garnish: corn kernels, diced cucumber, or grated Parmesan cheese.

MAKES 6 TO 8 SERVINGS

3 tablespoons extra-virgin olive oil
1 yellow onion, peeled and diced
1 leek, thinly sliced
2 garlic cloves, minced
2 bunches asparagus stalks (2 pounds), cut into ¼-inch pieces
4 cups water or Vegetable Stock (page 30)
1 cup heavy cream
Salt and freshly ground black pepper to taste
Corn kernels, diced cucumber, or grated Parmesan cheese, for garnish (optional)

In a large pot over medium heat, heat the olive oil and sauté the onion, leek, and garlic until soft, about 3 minutes. Add the asparagus and water or stock, and bring to a boil. Simmer for 25 minutes, or until the asparagus is tender. Transfer to a food processor or blender and puree in batches. Return to the pot and stir in the cream, salt, and pepper. Simmer until hot. To serve, ladle into heated soup bowls and sprinkle with a garnish.

NOTE: *This soup can be stored, in an airtight container, in the refrigerator for 2 to 3 days, or in the freezer for up to 2 months. Defrost and heat before serving.*

CHAPTER FOUR

*

SALADS

Today salads are a much-loved American obsession and creativity abounds in their preparation. If I could only have one course for dinner, salad would be it. I love its versatility and I love to play with textures, combining crisp, raw vegetables and greens with soft grains, fruit, cheese, hard-boiled eggs, or leftover fish or chicken. I just let my imagination take over and discover endless combinations.

Best of all, you can often whip up a salad just by combing through your refrigerator. In fact, that's how I created many of the recipes in this chapter. And when time is precious, it's great to know that this is one course you can improvise.

Although salads can be healthful, they can also be high-calorie if you're not careful. It's best to avoid bottled dressings, as many contain preservatives or unnecessary extra fat. Remember, it takes only 5 minutes to make a zesty balsamic vinaigrette from scratch.

My husband, Marvin, often cooks with me, and so several of his most terrific recipes appear in this chapter. For a hearty salad that invokes good old-fashioned memories of *gribenes* (chicken skin, deep fried in chicken fat until crisp), try the Hot Chicken Liver Salad, sprinkled with crispy, crumbled chicken skin. Marvin also takes a lighter route in his colorful Improv Salad, which combines bell peppers, fennel, corn, and arugula.

I like to dress up a simple salad by giving it an elegant presentation. My Layered Salad is served in long-stemmed martini glasses and always elicits admiration from dinner guests. While Bettina's Beet and Parmesan Salad has simpler visuals, it's also elegant because of the sophisticated ingredients—roasted beets sprinkled with olive oil and savory coriander topped with ultra-thin slices of Parmesan cheese.

SALADS

TIPS FOR SALADS

- Make salad dressings strong, so that a thin coating on greens will be enough.
- To check the seasoning in a dressing, dip a lettuce leaf into it and taste it.
- Use only enough dressing lightly to coat the greens; you can always add more dressing, but you can't take it away.
- For a well-seasoned vinaigrette, dissolve the salt in the vinegar before whisking in the oil. Double or triple the recipe so you'll have extra vinaigrette to use as a marinade for chicken or meat. Store in the refrigerator for up to 2 weeks.

ABOUT SALAD DRESSINGS

Two main ingredients go into most salad dressings: oil and vinegar, and they should be of excellent quality. The proportions vary according to the greens you use. Sometimes lemon juice is more suitable than vinegar because its accent is more subtle. Often the addition of a clove of garlic, shallots, or a sprinkling of a fresh herb will give the dressing a distinctive flavor. Acidic greens, such as spinach, watercress and curly endive, will need more vinegar in proportion to olive oil, while buttery greens, like bib, Boston, and loose-leaf lettuce, should be dressed with a milder proportion. Cooked vegetables, such as cauliflower, broccoli and green beans, are often more interesting when seasoned with a lemon-based dressing. Never drown your salad with dressing, and always add it at the last minute or pass it separately so each guest can add just the right amount for his/her taste (or diet).

QUICK CAESAR SALAD

Create your own Caesar salad in minutes without a recipe. To make a quick Caesar salad, toss assorted greens (romaine, radicchio, red leaf, or iceberg lettuce) in a large bowl and add a generous amount of grated Parmesan cheese, chopped anchovies, olive oil, and pepper. Taste before adding salt since the cheese and anchovies are very salty.

LAYERED SALAD

MICHEL RICHARD, chef-owner of Los Angeles's Citrus restaurant, created this salad for us. What a presentation this makes! A large martini glass is filled with layers of finely diced cucumber, tomatoes, avocado, and lettuce, and then sprinkled with chopped olives. It's amazing how a long-stemmed glass can transform an everyday salad into gourmet greens.

MAKES 4 SERVINGS

1 large cucumber, peeled and cut into ¼-inch dice

2 large tomatoes, cut into ¼-inch dice

1 avocado, cut into ¼-inch dice

1 cup finely shredded lettuce

½ cup minced black olives

4 teaspoons extra-virgin olive oil

8 teaspoons rice wine vinegar

4 basil leaves, for garnish

Place the prepared vegetables in separate bowls. Just before serving, fill martini glasses by carefully spooning a ½-inch layer each of cucumber, tomatoes, avocado, lettuce, and olives. Drizzle 1 teaspoon olive oil and 2 teaspoons rice wine vinegar over the top of each serving and garnish with 1 basil leaf.

BETTINA'S BEET AND PARMESAN SALAD

ONCE WHEN we visited our friends Bettina and Wolfe Rogosky in Italy, they served us this Tuscan salad in the garden of their house. Its rustic simplicity and bold taste dazzled us.

MAKES 4 SERVINGS

2 bunches (12 small) boiled or roasted beets, peeled and thinly sliced (page 51)
½ small yellow onion, peeled and thinly sliced
¼ cup extra-virgin olive oil
Juice of 1 lemon
Kosher salt and freshly ground black pepper to taste
Whole coriander, crushed or ground
Shaved Parmesan cheese (see Note)

Arrange the sliced beets on a large platter in a single layer. Top with onion slices. Sprinkle with olive oil, lemon juice, salt, pepper, and coriander. Just before serving arrange shaved Parmesan cheese over the beets.

NOTE: *The best way to shave Parmesan cheese is with a potato peeler.*

COOKING BEETS

In European open-air markets, precooked beets are often available, which is a great time-saver. In America we're not usually that lucky. So to save time, buy small beets, which are sweeter and cook in much less time than larger beets.

To roast, preheat the oven to 400°F. Remove the beet tops, leaving about ½ inch of stem and wash the beets. Place the beets on a large sheet of aluminum foil; pour ¼ cup water over them and seal by bringing the edges of the foil up over the beets and pinching the edges together to form a tent. Place on a baking sheet and bake for 45 minutes to 1 hour, depending on size, until the beets can be easily pierced through with a sharp knife. Remove from the oven, unwrap, and when cool enough to handle, peel the skin off and slice.

To boil, place the prepared beets in a heavy saucepan with water to cover. Cover tightly and boil for 30 to 45 minutes, depending on size, until the beets can be easily pierced through with a sharp knife.

WARM MUSHROOM SALAD WITH WILD GREENS

PREPARE THE greens in advance, but add the dressing just before serving. The produce sections of most supermarkets carry bags of prewashed and cut assorted greens—a valuable time-saver.

MAKES 4 SERVINGS

6 tablespoons extra-virgin olive oil

2 cups assorted mushrooms, cut in half

Salt and freshly ground black pepper to taste

3 cups mixed greens (arugula, radicchio, looseleaf), washed and torn into bite-size pieces

2 tablespoons balsamic vinegar

In a medium nonstick skillet, heat 2 tablespoons of the olive oil and sauté the mushrooms over medium heat until tender, about 5 minutes. Season with salt and pepper.

In a large bowl, toss the greens with the remaining olive oil and the vinegar. Season with salt and pepper. Arrange the greens on salad plates and spoon the warm mushrooms in the center.

MARVIN'S HOT CHICKEN LIVER SALAD

WE LIKE to prepare this salad just for the two of us as a main course. The inspiration for the crisp chicken skin that is sprinkled on this hot salad came from the delicious gribenes that I remember from my childhood. You can always poach the skinned chicken breasts for a salad.

MAKES 4 SERVINGS

1 small head Boston lettuce, torn into bite-size pieces
2 cups mâche (see Notes), torn into bite-size pieces
Skin of 2 chicken breasts
½ cup extra-virgin olive oil
1½ tablespoons balsamic vinegar
1 pound chicken livers, trimmed (see Notes)
Salt and freshly ground black pepper to taste

Wash the lettuces and dry on paper towels. Wrap them in the paper towels, place in plastic bags, and refrigerate for up to 3 hours.

Preheat the broiler; place the chicken skins on a foil-lined baking pan and broil until crisp, turning once, about 5 minutes. Drain on paper towels and set aside. Crumble when cool.

Just before serving, toss the lettuces with ¼ cup of the olive oil and the vinegar. Place on individual serving plates.

In a large skillet, heat the remaining ¼ cup olive oil. Season the chicken livers with salt and pepper, and sauté over high heat until lightly browned on both sides. Quickly transfer to a cutting board. Using a sharp knife, slice each chicken liver on the diagonal into 3 slices. Arrange the chicken livers on top of the prepared lettuce-lined plates. Sprinkle with the crisp crumbled chicken skin. Serve warm or at room temperature.

NOTES: *Mâche is a salad green also known as lamb's lettuce or corn salad. These dark green leaves form rosettes and add a soft, buttery flavor to salads. Available in many supermarkets in the produce section. Livers should be prepared according to kosher dietary laws.*

CELERIAC SLAW (CELERY ROOT SLAW)

CELERY ROOT is a much overlooked vegetable, although it can usually be found in the produce section of supermarkets. The most popular way to prepare it is to make this slaw, but it is also delicious boiled and mashed with potatoes.

MAKES 4 SERVINGS

1 small celeriac (about 2 pounds)
½ cup mayonnaise
1 tablespoon Dijon mustard
1 teaspoon balsamic vinegar
1 tablespoon fresh lemon juice
2 tablespoons sugar
¼ cup minced chives or scallions
Salt and freshly ground black pepper to taste

Cut off the root of the celeriac and peel the thick outside layer; wash it and cut it in julienne strips (or use a food processor fitted with the grater blade). Transfer to a large glass bowl.

In a medium bowl, combine the mayonnaise, mustard, balsamic vinegar, lemon juice, and sugar. Add the chives, salt and pepper, and mix well. Add just enough of the mayonnaise mixture to coat the celeriac and toss. Cover with plastic wrap and chill for at least 15 minutes before serving.

NOTE: *To prevent discoloring, toss the slaw with the juice of 1 small lemon.*

SALMON SALAD WITH ORANGE MAYONNAISE

THIS SALAD was inspired by a large piece of sautéed salmon left over from a previous night's dinner. It was delicious but tastes even better in this salad with the fresh, crisp addition of cucumber.

MAKES 4 SERVINGS

Orange Mayonnaise (below)
2 cups arugula
2 small cucumbers, thinly sliced into rounds
¼ cup extra-virgin olive oil
Salt and freshly ground black pepper to taste
½ pound cooked salmon, cold and cut into 1-inch pieces (page 112)
1 yellow onion, peeled and thinly sliced

Prepare the Orange Mayonnaise.

Coarsely chop the arugula and place in a medium bowl with the cucumber. Just before serving, toss with ½ of the olive oil, to moisten, and salt and pepper to taste. Arrange on salad plates and place the salmon pieces on top.

In a small nonstick skillet, heat the remaining olive oil and sauté the onion over medium heat until golden brown, about 2 minutes. Spoon over the salmon. Serve with Orange Mayonnaise on the side.

ORANGE MAYONNAISE

MAKES 1 ¼ CUPS

1 cup mayonnaise
1 tablespoon fresh orange juice
2 tablespoons grated orange zest

In a small bowl, mix together the mayonnaise, orange juice, and orange zest. Cover with plastic wrap and refrigerate until ready to serve. This will keep for 2 or 3 days in the refrigerator.

MARVIN'S IMPROV SALAD

THIS IS one of my husband Marvin's "whatever-is-in-the-fridge" inventions. One time he included some leftover borlotti beans we had enjoyed at lunch the previous day. This salad is never the same, because it depends on the season and, of course, what's on hand in the refrigerator—for example, diced or julienned daikon radish, red radishes, celery, carrots, cucumbers, and tomatoes.

MAKES 4 SERVINGS

1 large red bell pepper, diced
½ large fennel bulb, diced
1 large fresh ear of corn, kernels removed, or ½ cup frozen corn kernels, thawed
¼ cup extra-virgin olive oil
1 teaspoon balsamic vinegar
Salt and freshly ground black pepper to taste
2 cups thinly sliced arugula

In a large bowl, toss the red bell pepper, fennel, and corn kernels. Next, toss in 2 tablespoons of the olive oil, balsamic vinegar, and salt and pepper. In another bowl, toss the arugula slices with the remaining olive oil, salt, and pepper.

To serve, spoon the arugula in the center of each salad plate, spreading it out. Spoon the red bell pepper mixture in the center of each plate, piling it high, and serve.

BISTRO LEEK SALAD WITH MUSTARD VINAIGRETTE

NOTED LOS Angeles chef Michel Richard created this leek salad for Citrus Bistro, a casual café tucked inside his signature Citrus restaurant. This is my favorite bistro salad. Serve it hot or cold.

MAKES 4 SERVINGS

Mustard Vinaigrette (below)
6–8 small leeks, roots and outer layers removed, cleaned
1 cup Vegetable Stock (page 30) or Pareve Chicken Stock (page 33)
1 small tomato, finely diced
2 tablespoons minced fresh parsley
1 hard-cooked egg, white and yolk chopped separately

Prepare the Mustard Vinaigrette.

Clean the leeks and cut into halves or quarters lengthwise, depending on the size. In a large skillet, bring the stock to a boil, add the leeks, and simmer for about 10 minutes, or until tender when pierced with a fork. Drain and reserve the leek stock. Cool.

To serve, arrange the leeks on serving plates. Carefully spoon the diced tomato across the leeks in a thin strip. Repeat with the parsley, next to the tomato, then spoon a line of hard-cooked egg next to the parsley. Spoon the vinaigrette around the edges of the plate and over the leeks. Serve.

MUSTARD VINAIGRETTE

MAKES ABOUT ¾ CUP, OR 4 SERVINGS

1 teaspoon Dijon mustard
1 tablespoon red wine vinegar
2 tablespoons reserved leek stock or water
1 hard-boiled egg yolk
½ cup extra-virgin olive oil

continued

In a small glass bowl, combine the mustard, vinegar, and leek stock; whisk until smooth. Mash the egg yolk through a fine strainer and add to the mixture; whisk in the oil. Cover with plastic wrap and refrigerate. The vinaigrette will keep for several days in the refrigerator.

HARD-BOILED EGGS

For perfect hard-boiled eggs that will peel easily and not have an unattractive ring around the yolks, place uncooked, uncracked eggs in a heavy saucepan with cold water to cover. Add 1 teaspoon salt, bring to a boil, and cover. Turn off the heat and keep covered for 10 minutes. Then run cold water over the eggs immediately, to cool. Mark each egg with a colored marker to identify it from uncooked eggs, transfer the eggs to a bowl, cover with plastic wrap, and refrigerate.

HOLIDAY TURKEY SALAD

HOLIDAY LEFTOVERS don't have to taste plain and dreary; liven them up with some fresh fruits and vegetables. This entrée is so satisfying; it's got a hint of sweetness and a lot of crunch.

MAKES 4 TO 6 SERVINGS

3 cups diced cooked turkey
3 scallions, thinly sliced
1 cup seedless grapes
1 cup diced celery
½ cup diced red bell peppers
2 medium apples, peeled and diced
½ cup chopped toasted pecans (page 101)
¾ cup mayonnaise
½ teaspoon curry powder
1 tablespoon fresh lemon juice
Salt and freshly ground black pepper to taste
1 large head radicchio, thinly sliced (2 cups)

In a large bowl, combine the turkey, scallions, grapes, celery, red bell peppers, apples, and pecans.

In a small bowl, blend the mayonnaise, curry powder, and lemon juice. Add to the turkey mixture and toss gently. Season with salt and pepper. Cover and refrigerate.

To serve, arrange the radicchio on serving plates, and spoon the turkey salad on top.

TUNA NIÇOISE SANDWICH

I WAS INSPIRED to create this recipe after testing a version of salad Niçoise at an Italian-Greek restaurant in Santa Monica, California. The restaurant's famous salad is so good, customers stand in line for hours to buy it.

You can follow this recipe exactly or make your own combinations with whatever you have in your refrigerator. Serve these sandwiches to friends when watching a football game or other television event. Just put the rolls and other ingredients in bowls and on platters and serve salad-bar style.

MAKES 4 SERVINGS

Balsamic-Mustard Vinaigrette (recipe follows)
4 large French rolls
4 small red or new potatoes, steamed and sliced
8 thin tomato slices
2 hard-boiled eggs, sliced (page 58)
8 green beans, steamed
1 small red bell pepper, thinly sliced
Salt and freshly ground black pepper to taste
One 6-ounce can solid white tuna in olive oil, drained and flaked
4 thin slices red onion
4 anchovy fillets, drained
4 large romaine lettuce leaves

Prepare the Balsamic-Mustard Vinaigrette.

Slice the French rolls in half lengthwise. Spread the vinaigrette on the bottom and top halves of the rolls. On the bottom half, arrange the sliced potatoes, tomato, hard-boiled eggs, green beans, red bell pepper, and salt and pepper. Arrange some tuna on the pepper slices, then add sliced red onion and an anchovy fillet; top with a lettuce leaf. Cover with the top half of the roll. Cut the rolls in half crosswise, and serve.

BALSAMIC-MUSTARD VINAIGRETTE

MAKES ABOUT ½ CUP

1 tablespoon Dijon mustard
1 tablespoon balsamic vinegar
3 tablespoons extra-virgin olive oil

In a small bowl, blend the mustard, vinegar, and olive oil. Cover with plastic wrap and refrigerate until ready to use.

HALIBUT SALAD SANDWICH

YOU'LL FORGET all about canned tuna when you taste this fresh halibut salad that doubles as a sandwich filling. The tender, flaky fish cooks in less than 10 minutes. Double the recipe and serve it as a salad one day and sandwiches the next.

MAKES 4 SERVINGS

2 tablespoons extra-virgin olive oil
1 pound halibut fillet, ¾ inch thick
½ cup mayonnaise
1 cup finely chopped celery
½ cup thinly sliced scallions (white part only)
1 tablespoon minced fresh dill
1 tablespoon fresh lemon juice
Salt and freshly ground black pepper to taste
8 slices whole grain bread
Lettuce, for garnish

In a medium nonstick skillet, heat the oil over medium heat, and sear the halibut until brown on both sides, 6 to 10 minutes. Set aside to cool, then cut into 1½-inch pieces.

In a medium bowl, mix together the mayonnaise, celery, scallions, dill, and lemon juice. Fold enough of the mayonnaise mixture into the halibut to moisten it. Season with salt and pepper, and refrigerate at least 1 hour before serving.

Serve as a sandwich filling on whole grain bread, topped with lettuce, or serve as a salad.

SWEDISH CUCUMBER SALAD

THIS LIGHT, refreshing side dish makes a delightful accompaniment to cold poached salmon, broiled fish, such as sea bass or halibut or a melted cheese sandwich. Try it instead of cole slaw or potato salad. It takes only 5 minutes to make with the help of your food processor.

MAKES 4 SERVINGS

½ cup sour cream

2 tablespoons white wine vinegar

1 tablespoon sugar

3 tablespoons minced fresh parsley

2 tablespoons minced fresh dill

2 tablespoons thinly sliced scallions

4 cups unpeeled cucumbers, thinly sliced

Salt and freshly ground black pepper to taste

1 small head lettuce, sliced

In a medium bowl, mix the sour cream, vinegar, sugar, parsley, dill, and scallions until well blended. Add the cucumbers and toss gently. Add the salt and pepper. Cover with plastic wrap and chill at least 20 minutes. Serve on a bed of lettuce.

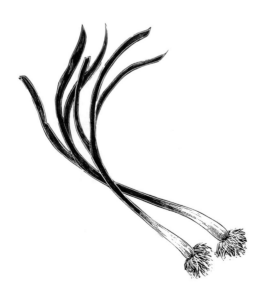

CHAPTER FIVE

*

VEGETABLES

MOST days of the week, a farmers' market can be found in Santa Monica, Malibu, Westwood, Beverly Hills, North Hollywood, and other parts of Los Angeles. These markets are much like the ones in small European villages. Shopping often takes 1 to 2 hours, as it's fun to stroll between the myriad colorful stands offering a variety of vegetables, fruits, cheeses, eggs, breads, and even beautiful flowers and plants. (And you'll hear more foreign languages spoken than English.)

Even people who don't enjoy shopping can become market enthusiasts, because of the people-watching and social activity that take place. Stop for a cup of espresso or freshly squeezed juice; sample an apple, grapefruit, or orange that a grower hands out to passersby. Sometimes you get to taste a wonderful slice of freshly baked whole grain bread.

Since the produce is so fresh, it will often keep for a week in the refrigerator, making it possible to buy enough fruits and vegetables to plan meals for several days. When planning your menu, don't get your heart set on one specific vegetable. Keep an open mind and look for fruits and vegetables that look the freshest. We always return home with bags of vegetables, ready to be tossed in a salad with greens, or sautéed with olive oil and garlic and served hot.

When vegetables are steamed rather than boiled, they remain beautifully crisp and tender. Surround a fish, chicken, or meat dish with colorful steamed vegetables, and it will resemble a garden on a plate. For a main course, try serving an array of steamed, grilled, or roasted vegetables. Vegetarian plates are a new feature on the menu at most fashionable restaurants today. Usually if there isn't one listed, a chef will be happy to serve a special veggie dish or make up a plate from side dishes that are available.

I am particularly proud of the recipes in this chapter. Spinach with Anchovies and Pine Nuts is one of those great side dishes you really can make in 5 minutes. My potato latkes are so different from most others because they're spread with chopped black and green olives, drizzled with olive oil, and served in wedges. And I cannot say enough good things about Marvin's Fresh Corn Polenta, not because Marvin is my husband (although that's a good reason), but because it's made with fresh corn kernels rather than ground cornmeal. Wait until you taste the difference.

If you are fortunate to have extra space in your backyard, put it to use as a garden. It's such a luxury to have your own garden, even a small one, as it can be a lifesaver when you're too tired to stop at the market after work. Picking a few fresh herbs and vegetables can work magic when added to the staples you already have on hand.

VEGETABLE GARNISHES

I love spending time in the kitchens of our friends' restaurants to learn some of their techniques and secret ingredients. The last time we visited Italy we stayed with the Brovelli family, who own and run Ristorante Il Sole in Lake Maggiore. I watched their son, Chef Davide Brovelli, prepping for dinner. He julienned carrots, zucchini, celery, and green onions, and ladled boiling water over the vegetables to soften them. Just before serving a salad, soup, or entrée, he garnished the course with this mixture. It was the perfect complement for every dish.

Garnishes are magical; they can enliven even the simplest dish. Davide's bowls of blanched colorful vegetables definitely gave each dish eye appeal. Don't be afraid to get creative.

VEGETABLES

Vegetable Garnishes

Poached Leeks

Gerri Gilliland's Colcannon (Mashed Potatoes and Green Cabbage)

Gerri's Potato Secrets

Potato Latkes with Chopped Olive Spread

Candied Sweet Potatoes

Spinach with Anchovies and Pine Nuts

Baked Eggplant with Tomatoes and Onions

Kathy's Green Beans

Fresh Fava Beans

Fresh Beans in Season

Marvin's Fresh Corn Polenta

Pan-Roasted Onions with Balsamic Glaze

Green Tomato Marmalade

Balsamic Glazed Carrots

Baked Stuffed Squash Blossoms

Asparagus with Tomato Confit

Cauliflower with Olive Oil and Garlic

Perfectly Cooked Cauliflower

POACHED LEEKS

LEEKS ARE delicious and so versatile. They make a great addition to soups and sauces, can be served hot or cold by themselves, or combined with lentils or any other vegetables. To select leeks, make sure the core or center is soft. If it is hard, this means that the leek is old and beginning to flower.

MAKES 4 SERVINGS

8 medium leeks, whole or sliced in half lengthwise
2 cups Vegetable Stock (page 30)
Salt and freshly ground black pepper to taste

Trim off the roots, coarse green tops, and outermost layers of the leeks. Wash or soak in cold water to remove any dirt.

In a large saucepan, over high heat, bring the stock to a boil. Reduce the heat, add the leeks, salt, and pepper and simmer, covered, until the leeks are tender when pierced with a fork, about 10 minutes. Arrange on heated serving plates. Bring the stock to a boil and boil until thick. Spoon over the leeks.

GERRI GILLILAND'S COLCANNON
(MASHED POTATOES AND GREEN CABBAGE)

THE **IRISH** lost out when Gerri Gilliland moved to Los Angeles from north-ern Ireland in the mid-1970s. While on holiday, she stepped off a Greyhound bus and never went back.

Gerri, the chef-owner of Gilliland's Café in Santa Monica, California (where she serves not only Irish cooking but eclectic food as well), is a good friend and was delighted to be a guest chef on my TV show, *Judy's Kitchen*. One of the dishes she prepared was colcannon; real comfort food. Colcannon is also great for breakfast, browned in the oven and served with a poached or fried egg.

MAKES 4 SERVINGS

4 medium russet or White Rose potatoes, peeled and cut into 1-inch chunks
Salt to taste
Water to cover potatoes
3 tablespoons nondairy margarine
6–8 scallions, trimmed and sliced
4 cups sliced Napa or savoy cabbage, sliced
Freshly ground black pepper to taste

In a large pot over high heat, combine the potatoes with salted water and bring to a boil. Reduce the heat to medium low and simmer, partially covered, for 10 to 15 minutes, or until tender. While the potatoes are still warm, put them through a ricer or a potato masher into a large bowl or mash them with the back of a large fork.

While the potatoes are boiling, prepare the cabbage. Heat 2 tablespoons of the margarine in a large nonstick skillet over medium heat, and sauté the scallions until tender, about 2 minutes. Add the cabbage, stir, cover, and wilt the cabbage about 15 minutes until it turns bright green. Add the cabbage mixture to the mashed potatoes and toss to combine completely. Season with salt and pepper, and top with the remaining 1 tablespoon margarine and mix well. Serve imme-diately.

- Add a little white vinegar to the water when boiling potatoes; the acidity helps the potatoes cook evenly and prevents them from falling apart.
- To remove moisture from boiled potatoes, drain them, return them to the pot, cover the pot with a towel, then cover with the lid. Place the potatoes over very low heat. Any moisture will evaporate but watch the pot carefully so the potatoes do not burn.
- Use russet potatoes for colcannon because they contain more starch to thicken the mixture naturally.

POTATO LATKES WITH CHOPPED OLIVE SPREAD

IT'S HARD to imagine Hanukkah without potato latkes. However, these have a fresh new look. They are fried in 6-inch rounds in fragrant olive oil, spread with a chopped olive mixture, cut into wedges, and drizzled with more olive oil.

MAKES 8 SERVINGS

2 large russet potatoes, peeled and shredded
1 tablespoon freshly squeezed lemon juice
1 egg
5 tablespoons extra-virgin olive oil plus extra, for drizzling
1 teaspoon salt
Freshly ground black pepper to taste
2 cups Chopped Olive Spread (recipe follows)

Place the shredded potatoes in a large bowl and add the lemon juice, egg, and 1 tablespoon of the olive oil, and season with salt and pepper. Mix well. Drain the liquid that accumulates.

In a 6-inch nonstick skillet, heat 2 tablespoons olive oil. Spoon half of the potato mixture into the hot oil and gently flatten with a fork or spatula, spreading evenly.

Cook over medium heat until brown on one side, about 5 minutes. Turn the latke carefully and brown on the other side. Drain on paper towels. Repeat with the remaining olive oil and remaining potato mixture.

Arrange the latkes on a serving platter. Spread 1 cup Chopped Olive Spread over each. Sprinkle with additional olive oil. Cut each latke into 4 wedges.

CHOPPED OLIVE SPREAD

MAKES ABOUT 2 CUPS

1 cup pitted black olives
1 cup pitted green olives
1 tablespoon extra-virgin olive oil
2 tablespoons minced fresh parsley

Coarsely chop the olives and place in a bowl. Add the olive oil and parsley, and toss well.

CANDIED SWEET POTATOES

No **NEED** to parboil sweet potatoes before baking. Just toss them with apple juice, brown sugar, and honey, then bake and serve. Perfect for Thanksgiving or any family feast. When I serve this dish for Passover, I replace the dark brown sugar with an additional ½ cup honey.

MAKES 8 SERVINGS

6 medium sweet potatoes (about 3 pounds)
1 cup apple juice
½ cup dark brown sugar
½ cup honey

Preheat the oven to 375°F.

Peel the sweet potatoes and slice them into 1-inch rounds. Place the rounds in a single layer in an ovenproof glass baking dish. Pour in the apple juice; sprinkle evenly with brown sugar and spoon the honey over the sweet potatoes. Cover with foil and bake for 20 to 30 minutes, turning after 15 minutes, until the potatoes are soft and glazed.

SPINACH WITH ANCHOVIES AND PINE NUTS

SPINACH IS a much misunderstood vegetable. Fresh spinach is available year round, and buying it frozen is a mistake that many people make. When my husband and I return from the open-air market, it's the first vegetable that we prepare for lunch. Just steam the spinach, drain, and add salt and pepper, or sauté it in fruity olive oil and minced garlic, and add tangy anchovies and toasted pine nuts. Follow the directions below and you will have glorified spinach in less than 5 minutes.

MAKES 4 SERVINGS

3 bunches fresh spinach
⅓ cup seedless yellow raisins, plumped in white wine
¼ cup toasted pine nuts (page 101)
¼ cup extra-virgin olive oil
2 tablespoons minced fresh parsley
4 anchovy fillets, cut into tiny pieces
Salt and freshly ground black pepper to taste
Pinch of nutmeg

Remove the large stems from the spinach leaves and wash the leaves in a large bowl filled with cold water. Sand will settle to the bottom. Transfer the spinach to a colander and, if necessary, repeat the washing with cold water, changing the water 3 or 4 times.

Place the spinach in a saucepan or steamer with just the water clinging to the leaves. Simmer for about 5 minutes, just until wilted. Drain thoroughly and chop fine. Place in a bowl.

Add the drained raisins and the pine nuts to the spinach, mixing carefully.

In a skillet or saucepan, over medium heat, heat the olive oil, add the parsley and anchovies. Stir over low heat for 2 to 3 minutes until the anchovies are soft. Add the spinach mixture, stir, cover pan, and sauté over low heat for 5 minutes to blend the flavors. Season with salt, pepper, and nutmeg.

BAKED EGGPLANT WITH TOMATOES AND ONIONS

THE INSPIRATION for this dish came from an eggplant I discovered in the refrigerator and the always-on-hand onion and tomato. Eggplant is a very versatile vegetable—you can puree, fry, or bake it. Many calories are saved by baking eggplant because when fried it soaks up oil like a sponge. The fresh flavor of the onion and tomatoes makes it taste like a ratatouille, with the same mellow flavors but prepared in much less time.

MAKES 4 SERVINGS

2 medium eggplants (about 2 pounds), cut in half lengthwise
¼ cup extra-virgin olive oil
2 garlic cloves, minced
1 cup diced yellow onion (about 1 medium)
2 cups diced tomatoes (about 3 medium)
Salt and freshly ground black pepper to taste

Preheat the oven to 375°F. Generously oil a nonstick baking sheet or line a baking sheet with foil and generously oil the foil.

Place the eggplant halves, cut side down, on the baking sheet and bake in the oven for 20 minutes, or until tender.

While the eggplant is baking, heat the oil over medium heat in a nonstick skillet, and sauté the garlic, onion, and tomatoes until tender, about 5 minutes. Add salt and pepper.

To serve, place halves of baked eggplant in the center of 4 heated serving plates and spoon the tomato mixture on top. Serve immediately.

VARIATION: *For a dairy meal, sprinkle grated or sliced Parmesan or Swiss cheese on top of the tomato mixture and broil until the cheese begins to melt. Serve immediately.*

NOTE: *Peeling the eggplant after roasting keeps the color of the meat light.*

KATHY'S GREEN BEANS

OUR DAUGHTER Kathy brought us some beautiful crisp green beans, fresh from her garden. I steamed them and then sautéed them in a skillet. Just before they were finished, I turned off the heat and left the pan partially covered. Prepared this way, they kept their bright green color.

MAKES 4 SERVINGS

1 pound green beans, ends trimmed
2 tablespoons extra-virgin olive oil
1 garlic clove, minced
Salt and freshly ground black pepper to taste

Place a steamer tray in a saucepan and add water to 2 inches deep. Bring to a boil and place the beans in the steamer tray. Steam, covered, for 5 minutes; reduce the heat to low and steam for 5 minutes more, or until beans are still semicrunchy and retain their green color. Turn off the heat and leave the pan partially covered; the beans will continue to steam. Do not overcook; watch closely and sample if necessary.

In a medium nonstick skillet, heat the olive oil and sauté the garlic for 1 minute. Add the steamed beans and, tossing with a wooden spoon to coat the beans with garlic, sauté for 2 minutes. Serve at once.

FRESH FAVA BEANS

WE MAKE this dish for lunch as often as we can find fresh fava beans at the open-air market. We like to have fun when we cook with them, and sometimes we'll fill espresso cups with the fava beans and spoon salmon roe on top.

MAKES 4 TO 6 SERVINGS

3½ pounds fresh fava beans, unshelled (about 4 cups shelled)
¼ cup extra-virgin olive oil or to taste
Salt and freshly ground black pepper to taste
Salmon roe, for garnish

Shell the beans, and put into a medium saucepan. Add water to cover, bring to a boil over high heat, and boil for 5 to 10 minutes, or until tender. Drain and remove the tough outer peel from the large fava beans. Spoon the beans into shallow bowls or espresso cups. Drizzle with olive oil, add salt and pepper, and spoon the salmon roe on top.

NOTE: *You can substitute borlotti beans or lima beans for the favas.*

FRESH BEANS IN SEASON

Fresh fava beans, lima beans, or cranberry (borlotti) beans make a great first course.

Every year we rent a house in Italy for two or three months, where we cook a lot with fresh produce, especially beans of all kinds. At home, when our grandchildren visit, we let them help shell the beans that we buy at the local farmers' market.

Beans, cold or hot, are a perfect complement for almost any menu. I like to add them to soups and salads, and they also go well with grilled meats. They are delicious served on their own as a first course with olive oil, salt, pepper, and fresh herbs, or with canned tuna as a salad. And any leftover cooked beans can be heated and mashed with a little oil and used as a sauce for pasta.

MARVIN'S FRESH CORN POLENTA

WHY BOTHER with ground cornmeal when you can use tender, fresh corn kernels and add healthful fiber to your polenta dish? The result is amazingly different and delicious.

8 ears fresh corn
Pinch of sugar or to taste
¾ cup grated Parmesan cheese
Salt and freshly ground black pepper to taste
Extra-virgin olive oil, for drizzling

Using a large, very sharp knife, and slicing from the top to the bottom of the cob, run the point of the knife down the center of each row of corn kernels. Using a large soup spoon or the back of the knife, leaving the corn kernel skin on, press in a downward motion, pushing the juice and pulp into a shallow bowl, to make about 2 cups. Add sugar to taste, depending on the sweetness of the corn.

In a medium nonstick skillet, sauté the pulp over medium heat, stirring constantly. Add ½ cup of the Parmesan cheese as it cooks until it thickens, 8 to 10 minutes. Season with salt and pepper.

To serve, spoon onto small serving plates. Sprinkle with the remaining Parmesan cheese and drizzle olive oil on top.

PAN-ROASTED ONIONS WITH BALSAMIC GLAZE

BALSAMIC VINEGAR is an ingredient that makes any dish speak Italian. This dish is an adaptation of a recipe of Chef Carlo Brovelli of Ristorante Il Sole on picturesque Lake Maggiore.

MAKES 6 SERVINGS

> 1½ pounds red or white pearl onions
> 2 tablespoons extra-virgin olive oil
> 1½ teaspoons salt
> ¼ teaspoon freshly ground black pepper
> 2 medium leeks
> ¼ cup balsamic vinegar
> 1 cup Vegetable Stock (page 30)
> 2 tablespoons unsalted butter or nondairy margarine
> ½ teaspoon chopped or minced fresh thyme

In a large saucepan, boil the onions with water to cover for 1 minute. Drain the onions, let stand until cool enough to handle, then carefully peel them, leaving roots and stem ends intact.

Transfer to a large bowl and toss with the olive oil, salt, and pepper.

Remove any damaged outer leaves from the leeks and all of the tough green parts. Cut the leeks lengthwise in half, leaving them attached at the root, and rinse them thoroughly of grit in cool running water. Cut crosswise into thin rounds.

In a large skillet, combine the onions, leeks, vinegar, stock, butter or margarine, and thyme, and cook over medium-high heat until the liquid reduces to a glaze, about 10 minutes. Serve hot.

GREEN TOMATO MARMALADE

IF **YOU** saw the movie *Fried Green Tomatoes*, you may think the only way to cook green tomatoes is to fry them. The truth is they also make a wonderful marmalade that's a perfect accompaniment to meat and poultry. Or serve the marmalade with hard Pecorino cheese at the end of a dairy meal.

MAKES 2 TO 4 CUPS

1½–2 cups sugar
½ cup water
2 pounds green tomatoes, diced (8 cups)
1 cup freshly squeezed orange juice
Grated zest of 1 orange and 1 lemon
10–15 mint leaves, sliced

In a large, heavy skillet, combine the sugar and water and bring to a boil, mixing constantly, until the sugar dissolves. Reduce the heat and simmer until the sugar begins to turn golden. Add the tomatoes, orange juice, and zests, and simmer until the tomatoes are soft and the liquid has reduced to a thick syrup, about 15 minutes. Mix in the mint leaves. Cool.

BALSAMIC GLAZED CARROTS

THIS SIMPLE and delicious no-frills recipe makes a wonderful side dish for chicken, turkey, or lamb. For an interesting twist, try substituting baby turnips for the carrots.

MAKES 4 SERVINGS

6 medium carrots (about ¾ pound), thinly sliced
¼ cup water
3 tablespoons unsalted butter or nondairy margarine
Salt to taste
3 tablespoons brown sugar
1 teaspoon balsamic vinegar

Place the carrots in a medium saucepan with the water, 1 tablespoon of the margarine, and a pinch of salt. Cover and simmer over low heat for 15 minutes, or until the carrots are just tender and the water is completely absorbed.

Meanwhile, prepare the sauce. In a small saucepan, combine the brown sugar, the remaining margarine, and the balsamic vinegar. Bring to a boil over medium-high heat and cook just until well blended, stirring constantly. Pour over the carrots and serve.

BAKED STUFFED SQUASH BLOSSOMS

IN **CALIFORNIA** from February through November, our local farmers' market sells beautiful zucchini squash blossoms. The blossoms are delicious stuffed with a duxelles of mushrooms, baked, and served as a first course.

MAKES 4 TO 6 SERVINGS

12 zucchini squash blossoms
4 tablespoons extra-virgin olive oil
½ cup minced onion
1 pound mushrooms, finely chopped
Salt and freshly ground black pepper to taste
Extra-virgin olive oil, for drizzling

Remove the pistils (the fuzzy yellow floret) from the center of the zucchini blossoms and discard. Set aside.

Preheat the oven to 325°F.

In a nonstick skillet, heat 2 tablespoons of the olive oil over medium-high heat; add the onions and sauté until soft, about 4 minutes. Add the mushrooms and cook, stirring with a wooden spoon, until cooked through and tender. Add the salt and pepper. Remove from the heat and set aside.

The easiest way to fill the blossoms is with a pastry bag fitted with a large round tip; otherwise, a spoon will do. Fill the bag with the mushroom mixture. Carefully open a squash blossom and insert the tip of the pastry bag. Squeeze the bag, allowing a small portion of the filling into the blossom; (about three quarters full) and gently squeeze the petals together at the top. Repeat the process with the remaining blossoms. Arrange the blossoms on a lightly oiled 10 × 12-inch baking dish that is large enough to hold the stuffed blossoms without crowding. (Can be prepared 1 hour in advance of baking.) Sprinkle with the remaining olive oil and season with salt and pepper. Cover with foil and bake for 20 minutes, or until tender. To serve, arrange on plates and drizzle with olive oil.

VARIATION: *For a dairy filling, fill the blossoms with a mixture of 1 cup ricotta, 1 egg, and minced basil to taste, and insert a 1-inch piece of mozzarella in each blossom.*

ASPARAGUS WITH TOMATO CONFIT

THE ASPARAGUS debate: thin asparagus or thick asparagus, which is the most delicious? The answer was very clear when we purchased thick (½ inch) round asparagus at our local Santa Monica outdoor market. We brought a bunch home and steamed them until tender; they were the best we'd ever eaten. These fat succulent stalks could replace a thick steak for me anytime.

MAKES 4 SERVINGS

Tomato Confit (below)
2 pounds asparagus, preferably jumbo
Salt and freshly ground black pepper to taste

Prepare the Tomato Confit.

Snap or cut the ends off the asparagus. If the stalks are fat, peel them with a potato peeler. Place the asparagus in a steamer tray over boiling water, cover, and cook until tender, 10 to 15 minutes, depending on the size of the asparagus. Remove from the heat immediately and serve with the Tomato Confit.

TOMATO CONFIT

MAKES ABOUT 1 CUP

2 tablespoons extra-virgin olive oil
1 small onion, peeled and finely diced
2 medium tomatoes, finely diced
2 garlic cloves, minced
Salt and freshly ground black pepper to taste

In a medium skillet, heat the olive oil over medium heat. Sauté the onion, stirring for 2 minutes. Add the tomatoes and garlic. Cook, stirring, for 4 minutes. Season with salt and pepper. Keep warm.

CAULIFLOWER WITH OLIVE OIL AND GARLIC

THE **BEST** ways to enjoy cauliflower are the simplest: steamed or sautéed, topped with Tomato Confit (page 83) or olive oil and salt and pepper. Don't toss the core of the cauliflower away, slice it and eat it raw like a carrot, or steam it along with the florets.

Once you experience the earthy fragrance, tender-crisp texture, and nutty-sweet flavor of a properly prepared cauliflower, any childhood memories of a pale, bumpy vegetable rendered mushy by overcooking will quickly fade.

MAKES 4 SERVINGS

1 medium cauliflower
¼ cup extra-virgin olive oil
4 garlic cloves, minced
Salt and freshly ground black pepper to taste

Wash the cauliflower and remove the outer leaves. Cut the florets away from the core. Cut the core into chunks. Break the florets into large bunches and place with the core in a steamer placed inside a saucepan. Fill the pan with water up to the steamer. Cover, bring the water to a boil, and boil until the florets are almost tender, about 10 minutes. Remove from the heat and let steam, covered, until a fork inserted in the cauliflower goes through easily.

In a nonstick skillet, heat the olive oil and garlic, about 1 minute. Add the florets and core, and sauté until lightly brown, turning once. Season with salt and pepper.

To serve, arrange on plates and serve as a first course or as an accompaniment to any main course.

PERFECTLY COOKED
CAULIFLOWER

- Choose compact white or ivory heads, free of brownish spots, with crisp, green leaves. Store, loosely wrapped in plastic wrap, in the vegetable bin of your refrigerator for up to 5 days.
- To prepare for cooking, remove the tough outer leaves. Break the florets that make up the head into bite-size clusters, or leave the head whole. The stalk is edible. Trim any discolored areas.
- Add a tablespoon of fresh lemon juice to the cooking water to help preserve the color and flavor.
- The best way to cook cauliflower is in a steamer over boiling water.

CHAPTER SIX

✳

PASTAS
AND
GRAINS

WHEN I was a child, I had never heard of pasta, but I knew all about *lukschen,* a Jewish word for egg noodles. Lukschen came in two shapes, the thin kind, which we added to chicken soup instead of matzah balls, and the wide variety, used in noodle kugels. And then there were *kreplach,* Jewish ravioli, made with egg-noodle dough and filled with cheese, potatoes, ground chicken, or kasha. Kreplach were boiled and served in soup, or fried and eaten as an appetizer or a side dish. When filled with cheese or potatoes, these delicious morsels were served with sour cream.

While I still like lukschen, my horizons have expanded to include all sorts of pasta, prepared in a multitude of fashions. I often make fresh pasta, as it cooks up quicker than the dried varieties. Pasta comes in many shapes and sizes. Many marry perfectly with vegetables; others are more harmonious with fish or meat. It's amazing how much the shape of the pasta affects the ultimate flavor of the dish.

In Pasta with Bell Peppers, Goat Cheese, and Basil, I use rotelle or fusilli. These curly shapes hold every kind of sauce. When I make an arugula sauce with vegetable stock and peperoncino, I toss it with penne.

Besides being an unabashed pasta lover, I consume a lot of grains, like millet, barley, rice, couscous, and bulgur. Sometimes I combine grains and beans to make hearty, healthful dishes that are especially attractive to vegetarians. I also add grains to soups and salads, or mix them with vegetables or fruits. Perhaps dishes like Brown Rice with Honeyed Apples, Polenta with Gorgonzola, and Vegetable Couscous will help convince you that making grains a part of your diet not only adds a lot of variety to your menus, but is fast, easy, and an economical way to cook.

Another plus is that most grains and pastas are quick-cooking, an important ingredient in 30-minute recipes.

PASTAS AND GRAINS

※

Pasta with Bell Peppers, Goat Cheese, and Basil

Penne with Arugula Sauce

Tagliatelle with Zucchini and Mint

Penne with Asparagus and Parmesan

Fusilli with Tuna Sauce

Bow-tie Pasta with Smoked Salmon Salad

Confetti Risotto

Risotto Latkes

Polenta with Gorgonzola

Polenta (Cornmeal)

Brown Rice with Honeyed Apples

Toasting Nuts

Mom's Red Rice

Vegetable Couscous

Matzah Gnocchi (page 179)

Holiday Sweet Potato Kugel (page 180)

PASTA WITH BELL PEPPERS, GOAT CHEESE, AND BASIL

PASTA SHAPES are not just intended to please the eye; many have a better reason for their existence. For example, tubular pasta demands a sauce that will cling to it, inside and out. Shells and dimpled shapes are exactly right for holding puddles of sauce. Twists allow a sauce to wrap itself around them, and they also work well in salads, tossed with a light vinaigrette.

MAKES 4 SERVINGS

2 tablespoons extra-virgin olive oil
2 garlic cloves, minced
½ cup finely chopped yellow onion
1 each red and yellow bell pepper, julienned (about 2 cups)
½ cup dry white wine
⅓ cup sliced pitted Kalamata or other brine-cured black olives
Salt and freshly ground black pepper to taste
½ cup finely shredded basil leaves
½ pound rotelle or fusilli pasta
3 ounces goat cheese, such as Montrachet, crumbled

In a medium nonstick skillet over medium heat, heat the olive oil and sauté the garlic and onion until soft, about 3 minutes. Add the bell peppers, sauté for 5 minutes, or just until tender. Add the wine and olives. Bring to a boil and cook until the wine is reduced by half. Season with salt and pepper, and stir in the basil.

In a large pot, bring salted water to a boil and cook the pasta until al dente. Drain well, reserving ½ cup of the cooking water.

In a large bowl, whisk 2 ounces of the goat cheese with the reserved cooking water until the cheese is melted and the mixture is smooth. Add the pasta and bell pepper mixture, and toss well. Sprinkle with the remaining goat cheese.

PENNE WITH ARUGULA SAUCE

THIS MARVELOUS dish was made for me by Lucio Pompili, chef-owner of Symposium, a Michelin one-star restaurant in Cartoceto, a city on the Adriatic coast of northern Italy. Arugula, with its peppery taste, is a popular and widely used salad green in Italy.

MAKES 4 SERVINGS

2 cups arugula, leaves only, discard thick stems
1 cup grated Parmesan cheese
1½ cups extra-virgin olive oil
6 tablespoons cold water
Salt and freshly ground black pepper to taste
½ pound penne (or any tube pasta), boiled and drained
2 tablespoon salmon roe, for garnish (see Note)

In the bowl of a food processor or blender, process the arugula until finely minced. Add 4 tablespoons of the Parmesan cheese, olive oil, and water, and blend until smooth. Season with salt and pepper. Transfer to a bowl and set aside.

Into a large pot, spoon ½ cup of the arugula sauce; add the drained pasta, top with the remaining sauce, and toss until completely coated.

To serve, spoon into heated shallow bowls and garnish with salmon roe. Serve with remaining Parmesan cheese.

NOTE: *Salmon roe can be found in the deli section of most supermarkets or gourmet stores.*

TAGLIATELLE WITH ZUCCHINI AND MINT

OUR NORTHERN Italian friends Maurizio and Francesca Rota made us this unusual mint-flavored pasta when we were visiting them. The mint grows wild in their garden, as it does in ours—so I was eager to try making this dish at home.

MAKES 8 SERVINGS

½ cup extra-virgin olive oil
2 medium zucchini, cut in half lengthwise and thinly sliced
1 red bell pepper, thinly sliced
Salt and freshly ground black pepper to taste
1 pound tagliatelle (or ½-inch-wide egg noodles or spaghetti)
1 cup cooking liquid or Vegetable Stock (page 30)
¾ cup minced fresh mint
1 cup grated Parmesan cheese

In a large skillet over medium heat, heat the olive oil and sauté the zucchini and red bell pepper until soft, about 5 minutes. Season with salt and pepper. Keep warm.

Cook the pasta in lightly salted boiling water until tender. Drain, reserving 1 cup of the cooking liquid. Add the pasta water or Vegetable Stock to the zucchini mixture and simmer. Add the pasta and toss with ½ cup of the mint and the Parmesan cheese until the pasta is completely coated with the zucchini mixture. Serve in heated serving plates and garnish with the remaining mint.

PENNE WITH ASPARAGUS AND PARMESAN

REACH INTO your Quick Fix Pantry (page 2) and if you find some dried pasta, you're in luck.

In Italy when asparagus is in season it is always exciting to see how many ways it can be served. In addition to accompanying pasta, asparagus is steamed and served with olive oil and lemon, or added to a frittata, or combined with risotto. But always served with grated or shaved Parmesan cheese.

MAKES 4 SERVINGS

¼ cup unsalted butter or margarine
3 garlic cloves, minced
1 pound asparagus, trimmed, cut diagonally into 2-inch pieces
Salt and freshly ground black pepper to taste
1 pound penne
1 cup freshly grated Parmesan cheese

In a large nonstick skillet, heat the butter. Add the garlic and asparagus and cook, stirring, until the asparagus is semifirm, about 5 minutes. Add salt and pepper.

Cook the penne in boiling salted water for 10 minutes, or until al dente. Drain and add to the asparagus in the skillet. Add ¼ cup of the Parmesan cheese. Add additional salt and pepper.

To serve, spoon into heated shallow bowls. Pass the remaining Parmesan cheese.

FUSILLI WITH TUNA SAUCE

THIS PASTA dish was inspired by the Italian classic vitello tonnato, which is thin slices of veal topped with a tuna sauce and served cold. Vitello tonnato is not considered kosher, since meat and fish cannot be served together, but this lovely dish offers much of the same flavor and is still in keeping with kosher cooking principles.

MAKES 4 SERVINGS

One 6-ounce can tuna, packed in oil
4 anchovy fillets, drained
2 tablespoons fresh lemon juice
½ cup extra-virgin olive oil
¼–½ cup Vegetable Stock (page 30)
2 tablespoons capers, washed and drained
1 tablespoon minced fresh parsley
Freshly ground black pepper to taste
½–¾ pound fusilli (see Note)

In the bowl of a food processor or blender, combine the tuna, anchovy fillets, and lemon juice, and blend until smooth. While the machine is running, add the olive oil in a thin stream and blend well. Transfer to a bowl and gradually stir in the stock, 2 tablespoons at a time, until the sauce is the consistency of light cream. Mix in the capers, parsley, and pepper. Transfer the tuna sauce to a large nonstick skillet, and bring to a simmer over low heat.

Cook the fusilli according to the package directions, drain; add to the tuna sauce, and mix well. Serve in shallow, heated bowls.

NOTE: *Each manufacturer's fusilli varies in shape. Some are a longer corkscrew and some are shorter and wider. For this recipe I selected the Latini brand of fusilli.*

BOW-TIE PASTA WITH SMOKED SALMON SALAD

STOREBOUGHT PASTA becomes an elegant dish when smoked salmon is added for color and flavor. This creamy pasta salad can be served hot or cold. It's perfect for a summer picnic or brunch, and tastes even better if made a day in advance. The salmon roe lends a particularly festive touch. Go light on the salt, since salmon and salmon roe tend to be salty enough for this dish.

MAKES 4 SERVINGS

One 12-ounce package bow-tie pasta, cooked al dente and drained

2 shallots or scallions, minced

3 tablespoons fresh lemon juice

2 tablespoons heavy cream

10 chives, cut into 1-inch pieces on the diagonal

¼ cup minced fresh dill

¼ pound smoked salmon, diced

Salt and freshly ground black pepper to taste

Salmon roe (optional)

In a large bowl, toss the cooked pasta with the shallots, lemon juice, cream, chives, and dill. Fold in the salmon. Add salt and pepper. Serve the salmon roe on the side or spoon it over the top, if desired.

CONFETTI RISOTTO

RISOTTO TAKES only 20 minutes to make from start to finish. This festive dish of many colors, which I created for a New Year's Eve party, looks like edible confetti. When the risotto is ready, serve it immediately from the pot into heated shallow bowls or it will become gummy and dry. If there is any risotto left over, you can make it into latkes (page 97) for a next-day meal.

MAKES 8 SERVINGS

Sautéed Confetti Vegetables (recipe follows)
3 tablespoons unsalted butter
1½ cups finely diced leeks, white and tender green parts, cleaned
2½ cups arborio rice (or short-grain pearl rice)
8 cups hot Vegetable Stock (page 30)
½ cup grated Parmesan cheese
¼ cup heavy cream
Salt and freshly ground black pepper to taste
2 tablespoons chopped fresh parsley, for garnish

Prepare the Sautéed Confetti Vegetables and keep warm.

In a large saucepan over medium heat, heat the butter and add the leeks. Cook until soft, about 5 minutes, add the rice and stir for 1 minute to coat with butter. Add 1 cup of the stock and continue cooking and stirring until the liquid is absorbed, about 2 minutes. Continue adding stock, 1 cup at a time, until all of it is absorbed; total cooking time is 18 to 20 minutes. Taste the risotto frequently toward the end of the cooking process (rice should be tender but not mushy or too soft). Just before the risotto is done, stir in the sautéed vegetables, Parmesan cheese, and cream, and stir gently to mix. Add salt and pepper. Serve in warm bowls and sprinkle parsley on top.

continued

SAUTÉED CONFETTI VEGETABLES

2 tablespoons unsalted butter or margarine
1 cup chopped carrots, cut into ⅛-inch dice
1 cup chopped zucchini, cut into ⅛-inch dice
1 cup chopped red bell pepper, cut into ⅛-inch dice

In a medium skillet over medium heat, heat the butter and sauté the carrots, zucchini, and bell pepper until tender but crisp, about 3 minutes. Keep warm.

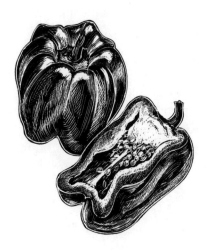

RISOTTO LATKES

IF YOU'RE lucky enough to have some risotto left over, you can use it to make crisp, cheese-flavored latkes in a very short time.

MAKES ABOUT 6 SERVINGS

½ cup chopped or grated mozzarella cheese
¼ cup freshly grated Parmesan cheese
2 tablespoons minced fresh parsley
1 cup packaged bread crumbs
2 cups leftover risotto (page 95)
½ cup extra-virgin olive oil
3 roasted red bell peppers (page 21), pureed

In a small bowl, combine the mozzarella and Parmesan cheeses, and parsley, and set aside.

Place the bread crumbs in a shallow bowl. Sprinkle your hands lightly with bread crumbs, scoop up 1 tablespoon of risotto in your hands, and shape it into a flat oval; make an indentation in the center of each oval with your thumb. Place 1 teaspoon of the cheese mixture in the center and cover the oval with another tablespoon of the risotto. Mold into 2- to 3-inch ovals, enclosing the cheese mixture completely. Roll in bread crumbs to coat.

In a nonstick skillet, heat the olive oil and fry the latkes, a few at a time, until crisp and golden brown on both sides. Using a slotted spoon, transfer them to paper towels to drain.

To serve, spoon the red pepper puree on serving plates and arrange the latkes on top.

POLENTA WITH GORGONZOLA

I ALWAYS HAVE trouble answering the question, "What is your favorite recipe?" But if I had to make a choice, I'd vote for this polenta, which I first sampled in a small restaurant above Lake Maggiore, Italy. I also like to serve the leftovers with sour cream (like mamaliga), or with maple syrup for the next day's breakfast.

MAKES 6 SERVINGS

Salt to taste
1 cup quick-cooking polenta (cornmeal) (page 99)
1 cup Gorgonzola or blue cheese, cut into pieces, at room temperature

In a large saucepan, bring 4 cups of water and salt to a boil. Add the polenta in a thin stream, and cook, stirring, about 15 minutes until thick, creamy, and soft.

Preheat the oven to 450°F.

Spoon the polenta into individual ovenproof baking dishes, top with Gorgonzola, and bake 5 minutes, or until cheese is soft and bubbly.

VARIATION: *Pour the polenta into an oiled pan and spread to a thickness of ½ inch. Cool until firm. Cut into 2-inch squares or diamond shapes. Place on a greased baking sheet and bake in the preheated (450°F) oven until crispy, about 10 minutes.*

Spread the polenta cutouts with Gorgonzola and toast in the oven for 5 minutes until cheese is soft and bubbly. Serve as an antipasto or a first course.

POLENTA (CORNMEAL)

The size of the grain used for making polenta affects its texture. Medium and coarse grinds work equally well. As a rule, the bigger the grain, the looser and more puddinglike the final result. Finer grains give a firmer and more compact polenta.

Most recipes for polenta require continuous stirring for hours, making it impossible to use in a quickly prepared meal. But with new, quick-cooking polenta available in most supermarkets, we can enjoy this delightful polenta in minutes instead of hours.

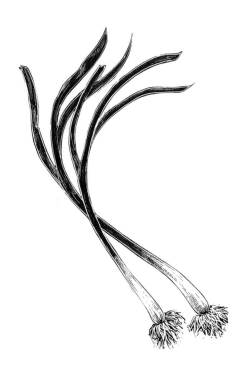

BROWN RICE WITH HONEYED APPLES

THE SPECIAL nutty flavor and chewy texture of brown rice make it a satisfying side dish for fish, poultry, and meat, or as an accompaniment to a vegetarian entrée. For a change of pace, try serving this honey-flavored brown rice with lamb chops or meat loaf.

MAKES 4 SERVINGS

1 cup quick-cooking brown rice

2 tablespoons extra-virgin olive oil

2 apples, peeled, cored, and finely diced (about 1½ cups)

¼ cup honey

½ cup coarsely chopped walnuts, toasted (page 101)

1 tablespoon grated orange zest, for garnish

Cook the rice according to the package directions. Heat the olive oil in a skillet over medium heat. Add the apples and honey. Simmer, stirring constantly, until the apples are tender but still hold their shape, about 5 minutes. Stir in the cooked rice and walnuts. Sprinkle with orange zest.

TOASTING NUTS

Toasting nuts enhances their flavor and makes them crisper. As soon as I purchase nuts, I store them in plastic bags in the freezer. When you are ready to toast the nuts, spread them in a single layer on a foil-lined baking sheet and bake at 350°F, turning or shaking them frequently, until the nuts are evenly browned, 5 to 10 minutes. Watch them carefully to make sure they do not burn. (See toasting hazelnuts, below.)

To add crunch to your favorite cakes, sprinkle finely ground nuts on oiled cake pans. This also prevents the cakes from sticking to the pans.

To toast hazelnuts (filberts): Spread a single layer of nuts on a foil-lined baking sheet and bake at 350°F, turning and shaking the pan frequently, until the nuts are evenly browned, 10 to 15 minutes. Watch them carefully, as they burn easily. Place the nuts in a soft towel and rub gently until most of the skins fall off.

MOM'S RED RICE

THIS IS a grown-up version of the old Spanish rice my mother used to make me when I was a child. Versatile and inexpensive, it's a foolproof accompaniment to meat or dairy menus. With a dairy meal, sprinkle rice with grated Parmesan cheese. Or for a meat meal, serve with Molly's Glazed Meat Loaf (page 150) and Kathy's Green Beans (page 75).

MAKES 6 SERVINGS

1½ cups quick-cooking long-grain rice
1 cup chopped tomato (1 large tomato)
1 cup diced yellow onion (1 medium onion)
¼ cup extra-virgin olive oil
⅓ cup canned tomato sauce
4 cups Vegetable Stock (page 30)
1 teaspoon salt to taste
Freshly ground black pepper to taste

Rinse the rice and soak in very hot water for 5 minutes. Drain thoroughly.

In a food processor or blender, puree the tomato and onion and set aside. In a saucepan over medium heat, heat the oil, then add the rice and sauté 1 minute. Stir in the tomato mixture and cook for 1 minute, mixing well. Add the tomato sauce, stock, salt and pepper, and mix well. Bring to a boil and simmer, covered, 3 minutes. Reduce the heat to low and cook the rice until tender, uncover and stir while cooking, about 15 minutes.

VEGETABLE COUSCOUS

HERE'S A fast, healthful idea for a Moroccan-inspired meal. Quick-cooking couscous is a real time-saver, and should be a pantry staple, as it's a refreshing change from rice or noodles.

MAKES 4 SERVINGS

2 tablespoons extra-virgin olive oil

2 garlic cloves, minced

1 large yellow onion, peeled and coarsely chopped

2 parsnips, peeled and thinly sliced

2 carrots, peeled and thinly sliced

One 8-ounce can tomatoes, drained, peeled, and cut into ¼-inch dice

Salt, and freshly ground black pepper to taste

½ teaspoon ground cumin

¼ teaspoon crushed red pepper flakes

1 cup Vegetable Stock (page 30)

1 small zucchini, cut into ¼-inch dice

½ cup canned chick-peas, drained

Couscous (recipe follows)

Fresh cilantro or parsley sprigs, for garnish

3 tablespoons sesame seeds, for garnish

In a large nonstick skillet over medium heat, heat the oil and sauté the garlic and onion until tender but not brown, about 5 minutes. Add the parsnips, carrots, tomatoes, salt, pepper, cumin, red pepper flakes, and the stock. Bring the vegetables to a boil. Reduce the heat to low, cover, and simmer for 10 minutes, or until vegetables are tender yet firm. Add the zucchini and chick-peas; cook just until zucchini is tender, about 10 minutes.

Meanwhile, prepare the couscous as instructed on page 104.

To serve, spoon some couscous on a warm plate; top with vegetables and some broth. Garnish with cilantro or parsley and sesame seeds.

continued

COUSCOUS

MAKES ABOUT 3 CUPS

1½ cups Vegetable Stock (page 30)
1 tablespoon unsalted nondairy margarine
1 cup quick-cooking couscous

In a large saucepan over medium-high heat, bring the stock and the margarine
to a boil. Add the couscous, cover, and remove from the heat. Let stand for 5
minutes. Fluff up with a fork.

CHAPTER SEVEN

*

FISH

I remember a time when all we ate was canned tuna and salmon instead of fresh fish. Years ago, fish formed only a small portion of our diet, but today we have all become attuned to the health benefits of consuming a lot of fish.

Since we eat more fish now than ever before, we need to know how to prepare it to enhance its delicate nature. Luckily for busy cooks, fish tastes so much better when its cooked quickly and simply. I love it sautéed, poached, grilled, or broiled.

If you do want to bake fish, be sure to do so in a hot oven (400° to 450°F), which seals in the flavor and reduces the cooking time. Fatty fish, such as salmon, takes best to this cooking method, but any fish will work as long as you bake it only until it's just cooked through and flakes lightly when cut with a fork. Never overbake fish; once it dries out, there's nothing you can do to resuscitate it.

Some of the best-tasting fish are kosher, such as ling cod, carp (a popular choice for making gefilte fish), snapper, trout, sand dabs, mackerel, salmon, perch, whitefish, tuna, and halibut. Such variety gives you much choice of preparation and recipes—I take full advantage and showcase a myriad of cooking styles in this chapter. For example, Halibut with Kumquats and Passion Fruit possesses a distinct Chinese influence, while Peppered Whitefish with Leeks and Red Wine Sauce is impeccably French. And Gramma Gene's Gefilte Fish recipe is an updated version of the traditional Jewish favorite.

Be sure to purchase the freshest fish possible. It's best to shop at markets where fish is the specialty. But if your only option is the nearest supermarket, select only fresh fish—*not* fresh-frozen and kept on ice. If you buy whole fish, look for clear eyes and bright pink or red gills. All fillets or steaks should have a bright, moist appearance with no discoloration, and a clean, fresh odor.

TO STORE FISH

- Rinse fish in very cold water and loosely wrap with waterproof paper, aluminum foil, or plastic wrap, and set in a container to collect any fluid loss.
- Store in the coldest part of the refrigerator. Or store in the refrigerator surrounded by finely crushed ice.
- If buying frozen fish, freeze it, unopened, in its original package.
- To freeze fresh fish, wrap in freezer paper or seal in freezer containers.
- Frozen fish should be thawed in the refrigerator in the morning or the day before it is needed.

FISH

To Store Fish

Peppered Whitefish with Leeks and Red Wine Sauce

Halibut with Kumquats and Passion Fruit

One-Side Sautéed Salmon

Teriyaki-Glazed Salmon Fillets

Fish Stew

Kerstin's Swedish Potato and Gravlax Casserole

Baked Codfish

Baked Roman Fish Timbale (Fillet of Sole Romana)

Baked Sea Bass with Black-Olive Sauce

Chilean Sea Bass with Tomato-Fennel Stew

Gramma Gene's Gefilte Fish (page 183)

PEPPERED WHITEFISH WITH LEEKS AND
RED WINE SAUCE

CLAUDE **S**EGAL, the chef of Los Angeles's acclaimed Drai's restaurant, is noted for his French cooking with a California flair. When Claude was a guest chef on my television show, *Judy's Kitchen*, he prepared this dish. I've never forgotten its delicious taste.

Much like pepper steak, whitefish is encrusted with black peppercorns and served on a bed of caramelized leeks. The piquant crust on the fish imparts only a hint of pepper to the delicate flesh. Use a good-quality wine for the sauce, and serve more red wine to drink with the fish.

MAKES **4** SERVINGS

3 tablespoons coarsely crushed black pepper
1½ pounds whitefish fillet, cut into 4 steaks
Salt to taste
6 tablespoons (¾ stick) unsalted butter
2 shallots, peeled and thinly sliced
1 cup dry red wine
1 cup hot Fish Stock (page 31)
Freshly ground black pepper to taste
Caramelized and Fried Leeks (recipe follows)

Place the crushed pepper in a shallow bowl or plate. Sprinkle the fish with salt and press the skin side into the crushed pepper. Set aside.

Melt 2 tablespoons of the butter in a medium skillet over medium heat and add the shallots. Sauté for 1 minute, then add the wine. Cook over high heat until the wine has almost evaporated. Stir in the fish stock and cook until the sauce reaches the consistency of a thick paste. Using a wire whisk, finish the sauce on low heat by adding small pieces of the remaining 4 tablespoons butter. Season with the ground pepper. Strain the sauce and keep warm.

Cook the peppered whitefish, skin side down, in a nonstick skillet over medium-high heat for 3 minutes. Turn and cook for 3 minutes more, or until done. Keep warm.

Prepare the Caramelized and Fried Leeks below.

To serve, spoon the caramelized leeks in the middle of each plate and arrange the whitefish on top, skin side up. Spoon the sauce around the fish and garnish with the fried leeks.

CARAMELIZED AND FRIED LEEKS

MAKES 4 SERVINGS

6 medium leeks
4 cups vegetable oil, for frying
Salt to taste
3 tablespoons unsalted butter
1–2 teaspoons sugar
¼ cup water
Freshly ground black pepper to taste

FOR FRIED LEEKS

Cut each leek in half lengthwise and soak in cool water for about 10 minutes. Cut one of the leeks into a thin julienne. Heat the oil in a deep-fryer or heavy pot with a metal strainer and quickly fry the julienned leeks until golden brown. Drain on paper towels and sprinkle with salt. Set aside.

FOR CARAMELIZED LEEKS

Cut the remaining leeks into 4-inch lengths. Melt the butter in a medium skillet over medium heat and add the leeks, sugar, water, salt, and pepper. Cook until the liquid has completely evaporated and the leeks are caramelized, about 5 minutes.

HALIBUT WITH KUMQUATS AND PASSION FRUIT

YUJEAN KANG, a talented Chinese chef, and his wife, Yvonne, own two restaurants in the Los Angeles area. Traditionally Yujean prepares this dish with catfish, which is not kosher. I asked him to substitute halibut and it works beautifully. Kumquats and passion fruit juice offer a contrast in flavors to this updated version of sweet-and-sour fish.

MAKES 4 SERVINGS

FOR THE FISH AND KUMQUATS

1 pound halibut fillet

2 tablespoons rice wine or dry white wine

1 teaspoon peeled and minced fresh ginger

Pinch of salt

Pinch of freshly ground black pepper

Sugar to taste

1 egg white, lightly beaten

2 tablespoons cornstarch

2 cups vegetable oil, for frying

3 cups silver sprouts (bean sprouts with ends trimmed)

½ each green, yellow, and red bell pepper, julienned

¼ cup dry white wine

3 kumquats, julienned

FOR THE PASSION FRUIT SAUCE

1 tablespoon chili paste

1 tablespoon peeled and minced fresh ginger

2 tablespoons rice wine

2 tablespoons Vegetable Stock (page 30)

2 tablespoons rice vinegar

2 tablespoons passion fruit juice

Pinch of salt

Pinch of sugar

1 tablespoon cornstarch mixed with ½ cup cold water

Cut the halibut crosswise into ¼-inch-thick slices. Julienne each slice into ⅛-inch strips. Place in a glass bowl, and toss with the rice wine, ginger, salt, pepper, and sugar. Coat with egg white and then with cornstarch. Marinate the halibut for about 2 minutes.

Pour 2 cups oil into the wok and heat to a medium temperature. Fry the halibut until barely cooked, about 2 minutes (almost like deep-frying but at a lower temperature). Transfer the halibut to the strainer, allowing the excess oil to drain. Set aside. Add the sprouts to the wok and stir for 1 minute. Add the bell peppers; stir, then add the wine and stir until the sprouts are cooked but still crisp, 2 minutes. Add to the fish in the colander. Top with the kumquats and set aside.

To make the sauce, add the chili paste, ginger, rice wine, stock, rice vinegar, passion fruit juice, salt, and sugar to the wok. Add the cornstarch mixture and simmer about 3 minutes, or until almost caramel in color. Return the halibut mixture to the wok and stir, coating evenly.

Spoon into a serving bowl. Serve immediately.

ONE-SIDE SAUTÉED SALMON

OF ALL the kosher seafood available in America, salmon is my favorite. When the salmon is sautéed on the skin side, the skin acts as a shield; the flesh never touches the pan, leaving it moist, tender, and slightly rare.

MAKES 6 SERVINGS

Green Butter Sauce (below)
One 3-pound fillet fresh salmon, scales removed, skin on, cut into 6 pieces
Salt and freshly ground black pepper to taste
¼ cup extra-virgin olive oil
2 tablespoons unsalted butter or margarine
2 cups mixed wild mushrooms, left whole if small, sliced in half if large

Prepare the Green Butter Sauce and keep warm.

Season the skinless side of the salmon with salt and pepper. Put a few drops of olive oil in a large nonstick skillet. Sauté the salmon over low heat, skin side down—do not turn—(adding additional olive oil if needed), for 10 to 15 minutes, depending on thickness. (A 1-inch-thick piece of salmon will be rare after 10 minutes.) While the salmon is sautéing, heat the butter and sauté the mushrooms in a medium skillet about 5 minutes, or until the mushrooms become soft. Keep warm.

Spoon the mushroom sauce onto warm plates, top with the salmon, and garnish with the mushrooms and remaining ¼ cup chives from the Green Butter Sauce.

GREEN BUTTER SAUCE

MAKES ABOUT 2 ½ CUPS

½ pound unsalted butter or margarine, cut into 4-ounce pieces, softened
1 cup chopped chives
½ cup chopped fresh parsley
1 tablespoon freshly squeezed lemon juice

¾ cup Vegetable Stock (page 30) or Fish Stock (page 31)
½ cup dry white wine
Salt and freshly ground white pepper to taste

In a food processor or blender, blend the butter, ¾ cup of the chives, and the parsley. Add the lemon juice. When the mixture is smooth and bright green, strain it through a fine sieve, using a spatula to push it through.

In a medium saucepan over medium heat, combine the stock and wine, and cook until the mixture is reduced in volume to ½ cup, about 10 minutes, and let cool slightly. Slowly whisk in the butter mixture, and season with salt and pepper; cover and keep warm until ready to use.

TERIYAKI-GLAZED SALMON FILLETS

THE GLAZE can be made in advance and reheated just before cooking the salmon. The gingerroot is a great addition to the sauce.

Most people think of teriyaki sauce as a marinade. In Japanese cuisine it is often used as a glaze for grilling or broiling meat and seafood; in this recipe it is used as both a marinade and a glaze.

MAKES 4 SERVINGS

5 tablespoons soy sauce

3 garlic cloves, minced

2 tablespoons fresh lemon juice

1 teaspoon sugar

Four 6-ounce salmon fillets, skin removed

1 tablespoon dry sherry

1 tablespoon Dijon mustard

1½–2 teaspoons peeled and grated fresh gingerroot or to taste

1 tablespoon honey

½ teaspoon white wine vinegar

1 tablespoon extra-virgin olive oil

In a resealable plastic bag or shallow glass baking dish, combine 2 tablespoons of the soy sauce, ⅓ of the minced garlic, lemon juice, and sugar. Add the salmon and marinate, sealed and chilled, for 15 minutes. Remove the salmon from the bag and pat dry with paper towels, discarding the marinade.

In a small saucepan, combine the remaining soy sauce and minced garlic, and the sherry, mustard, gingerroot, honey, and vinegar and bring to a boil. Reduce heat and simmer until glaze coats the back of a spoon, about 5 minutes.

In a heavy skillet, over moderate-high heat, heat the oil and sear the salmon on each side for 3 minutes, beginning skin side up.

To serve, arrange the salmon on serving plates and spoon the glaze over the salmon.

FISH STEW

THE FIRST time I prepared this stew I used ling cod and Mexican sea bass fillets, but the recipe works just as well with other fish combinations; try your own mixture. Since there is red wine in the sauce, serve red wine with this dish.

MAKES 4 SERVINGS

3 tablespoons extra-virgin olive oil
3 garlic cloves, minced
2 cups chopped yellow onions (about 2 medium)
1 cup chopped celery (about 2 stalks)
1 cup chopped fresh fennel
5 small tomatoes, diced (about 1 pound)
1 tablespoon tomato paste
2 tablespoons red wine vinegar
½ cup dry red wine
½ cup cold water
¼ cup minced fresh parsley
1 tablespoon sugar or to taste
1 tablespoon fennel seeds
Salt and freshly ground black pepper to taste
2 pounds fish, such as cod, sea bass, halibut, and red snapper fillets, cut into
*   1-inch dice*

In a large heavy pot over medium heat, heat the oil and sauté the garlic and onion for about 3 minutes until soft but not brown.

Add the celery and fennel, and sauté for about 3 minutes. Add the tomatoes, tomato paste, vinegar, wine, water, parsley, sugar, fennel seeds, salt, and pepper.

Let simmer for about 15 minutes. Add the fish, cover the pot, and cook for about 5 minutes, or until fish is cooked through but still firm. Serve immediately in heated shallow soup bowls.

KERSTIN'S SWEDISH POTATO AND GRAVLAX CASSEROLE

MY **SWEDISH** friend Kerstin Marsh is a great cook, and she serves this family specialty as a first course with papaya, cucumbers, and sesame crackers. A perfect addition to a bagel and cream cheese brunch.

MAKES 6 SERVINGS

Unsalted butter for the baking dish
Eight (1¾ pounds) white or red new potatoes, peeled, thinly sliced, and boiled
8 large slices gravlax or smoked salmon
½ small yellow onion, peeled and thinly sliced
2 tablespoons snipped fresh dill
Salt and freshly ground black pepper to taste
1½ cups warm heavy cream
3 tablespoons bread crumbs
2 tablespoons unsalted butter, cut into pieces

Preheat the oven to 400°F.

Brush an 8-inch square baking dish with butter. Arrange half of the sliced potatoes on the bottom. Arrange the slices of gravlax on top of the potatoes. Sprinkle with the onion and dill. Repeat with a top layer of the remaining sliced potatoes. Season with salt and pepper.

Pour the cream over the potato mixture. Sprinkle the bread crumbs and pieces of butter over the potatoes. Bake for 25 minutes, or until golden brown and cooked through. Serve hot or cold.

NOTE: *Whole, new unpeeled potatoes, steamed, take about 20 minutes to cook, depending on the size of the potatoes. Peeled and sliced potatoes, boiled, take only 5 minutes.*

BAKED CODFISH

COD REMAINS one of the world's most abundant and versatile foods. It's a lean, flaky white fish, modestly priced, and much neglected. Here's your chance to check out its virtues, enhanced with flavorful ginger, garlic, and lemon accents. If you like, substitute sea bass, halibut, or red snapper.

MAKES 6 SERVINGS

2 tablespoons extra-virgin olive oil
6 codfish fillets, 5 to 6 ounces each
6 thin slices ginger, peeled
6 thin slices unpeeled lemon, seeds removed
1 yellow onion, peeled and finely chopped
1 garlic clove, minced
Salt and freshly ground black pepper to taste
1 cup dry white wine
3 tablespoons unsalted butter or margarine

Preheat the oven to 375°F.

Rub a large baking dish with the olive oil and place the cod fillets in it. Top each fillet with a slice of ginger and lemon. Sprinkle with the onion, garlic, salt, and pepper. Pour the wine over the top. Cover with aluminum foil and bake for 12 minutes. Uncover the dish and spoon most of the cooking juices into a medium saucepan, leaving a little of the juices in the pan. Return the fish to the oven and bake for 10 minutes, or until the fish flakes easily. Meanwhile, bring the cooking juices to a boil over high heat. Whisk in the butter and boil until the sauce has thickened, about 5 minutes.

To serve, arrange the fillets on heated serving plates and pour the sauce over them. Serve with small steamed or boiled potatoes and a green vegetable.

BAKED ROMAN FISH TIMBALE
(FILLET OF SOLE ROMANA)

THIS DELICATE fish, a favorite of the Jews of Rome, is enhanced with layers of endive and bread crumbs. Carolee Blumin, my devoted recipe tester, loved this recipe so much that she made it a dozen more times.

MAKES 4 SERVINGS

1½ pounds fresh fillet of sole
5 tablespoons extra-virgin olive oil
½ cup fine dry bread crumbs
1 garlic clove, minced
1 pound (1 large head) curly endive or frisée, leaves coarsely chopped
Salt and freshly ground black pepper to taste

Preheat the oven to 350°F.

Rinse the fish under cold running water and pat dry with paper towels. Set aside.

Brush a 2-quart casserole around the bottom and sides with 1 tablespoon of the olive oil and sprinkle to coat evenly with about ¼ cup of the bread crumbs. In a large bowl, toss the garlic with the endive and salt and pepper. Spread a third of the greens in the bottom of the casserole. Top with half of the fish fillets, arranged like spokes of a wheel. Sprinkle salt, a generous amount of pepper, and a tablespoon of bread crumbs over the fish; then drizzle a table-spoon of olive oil on top.

Repeat with another layer of greens, and the remaining fish. Season with salt, pepper, and the remaining bread crumbs. Top the casserole with the remaining greens, salt and pepper, and the remaining olive oil.

Using a spatula, gently press the layers of greens and fish down into the casse-role. Bake, covered, for 20 minutes. Raise the heat to 425°F, then gently press the top layer down again and continue baking uncovered for 10 minutes. Serve hot or cold with Orange Mayonnaise (page 55).

BAKED SEA BASS WITH BLACK-OLIVE SAUCE

HANUKKAH CELEBRATES a miracle that is said to have occurred more than two thousand years ago. The lamp in the Holy Temple was relit with enough oil to last one day; somehow, it lasted for eight.

Few people know that the miraculous oil was made from olives. This recipe was part of a Hanukkah article I wrote for the *Los Angeles Times*. It uses chopped olives for the sauce with sea bass to serve during Hanukkah.

MAKES 4 SERVINGS

4 garlic cloves, minced
1 cup pitted black olives, chopped
1 teaspoon crumbled dried oregano
1 teaspoon crumbled dried basil
2 tablespoons fresh parsley, chopped
Salt and freshly ground black pepper to taste
¼ cup extra-virgin olive oil
2 pounds sea bass (4 to 6 fillets)
½ cup Vegetable Stock (page 30) or dry white wine

Preheat the oven to 425°F.

In a small bowl, combine the garlic, olives, oregano, basil, and parsley. Season with salt and pepper.

In a 13 × 9-inch glass baking dish, heat the oil for 1 minute. Spread the olive mixture evenly over the bottom of the baking dish. Arrange the sea bass, skin side up, on top. Pour the stock around the fillets. Bake, basting occasionally with juices, for 15 minutes, or until done.

To serve, arrange the fillets and olive mixture on heated serving plates.

CHILEAN SEA BASS WITH TOMATO-FENNEL STEW

THIS IS one of our favorite main courses to serve for dinner when we have guests. Chilean sea bass is one of those special fish that can never be overcooked. If it is not available or the price is too high, sea bass works fine.

MAKES 4 SERVINGS

Tomato-Fennel Stew (below)
Four 4-ounce sea bass fillets (preferably Chilean)
1 cup dry bread crumbs
Salt and freshly ground black pepper to taste
3 tablespoons extra-virgin olive oil

Prepare the Tomato-Fennel Stew.

Dip each fillet into the bread crumbs and coat the fillet. In a nonstick skillet, heat the olive oil and brown the fillets on both sides, about 5 minutes each side, depending on the thickness.

To serve, arrange each fillet in the center of a warm serving plate and spoon the Tomato-Fennel Stew over the fish. Serve immediately.

TOMATO-FENNEL STEW

MAKES ABOUT 3 CUPS

2 tablespoons extra-virgin olive oil
4 medium tomatoes, finely diced
1 fennel stalk, finely diced
1 cup fresh corn kernels
1 cup Vegetable Stock (page 30)
Salt and freshly ground black pepper to taste

In a nonstick skillet, heat the olive oil and sauté the tomatoes, fennel, and corn for 5 minutes. Add the stock and cook until it comes to a boil. Reduce the heat and simmer for 5 minutes. Season with salt and pepper. Keep warm.

CHAPTER EIGHT

✳

POULTRY

CHICKEN always brings up fond memories in my mind. In our house, when I was growing up, we eagerly looked forward to chicken soup and roast chicken every Friday night.

Although chicken is still a staple in our household today, it bears little resemblance to my childhood Friday-night version. Today, I often grill chicken breasts or high-heat-roast a cut up chicken stuffed with herbs (30-Minute Chicken for a Crowd) for a fast, delicious meal.

Sometimes I use poultry to lighten up a heavier entrée like chili. Quick Turkey Chili, flavored with cilantro and cumin, really fits in with the way we eat in the nineties. Poached chicken can also taste wonderful, particularly when gently simmered in a Ziploc bag, as in Ziploc Chicken Surprise. You can choose different vegetables to cook with the chicken, depending upon the season and what is market-fresh.

If you've never eaten guinea hen, you must try the recipe in this chapter. The quick-to-make honeyed Grand Marnier glaze really penetrates the meat and turns the skin a shiny, golden hue.

When I order chicken from the kosher butcher, I purchase an extra supply for the freezer, so that I always have poultry on hand. After all, what kind of kosher cook would I be if I couldn't make chicken soup at the drop of a hat?

CHICKEN

———— ✳ ————

POACHED CHICKEN BREASTS

30-MINUTE CHICKEN FOR A CROWD

GLAZED GUINEA HENS

QUICK TURKEY CHILI

TURKEY KEBABS WITH HONEY GLAZE

TURKEY SCHNITZEL

ZIPLOC CHICKEN SURPRISE

CHICKEN BREASTS IN PACKAGES

GRANDMA'S PICKLED CHICKEN

CHICKEN JAMBALAYA

MINCED CHICKEN IN LETTUCE WRAPPERS

CREOLE CHICKEN

COLD ROASTED CHICKEN WITH FENNEL AND LEEKS

JANIE MASTERS' RED WINE SAUCE

POACHED CHICKEN BREASTS

To make tender chicken breasts for salads and cold dishes, poach the breasts in simmering Chicken Stock (page 32) for 10 to 15 minutes, or until cooked through, depending on the size of the breasts. Cool them in the stock and chill, covered with a little of the stock.

30-MINUTE CHICKEN FOR A CROWD

ONE **ROSH** Hashanah, after spending hours in synagogue, I was faced with the task of feeding nineteen hungry people representing three generations. The easiest main course I could think of was this roasted chicken, which is a meal in itself.

MAKES ABOUT 16 SERVINGS

FOR THE STUFFING

¼ cup fresh rosemary, stemmed
¼ cup chopped fresh oregano
3 garlic cloves, peeled
Salt and freshly ground black pepper to taste

FOR THE CHICKEN

¼ cup extra-virgin olive oil
2 large yellow onions, peeled and diced
4 garlic cloves, minced
6 large carrots, peeled and diced
4 large zucchini, diced
Four 2½-pound chickens, cut into eighths
Rosemary and oregano sprigs
Salt and freshly ground black pepper to taste
1 cup dry white wine
1 cup Chicken Stock (page 32)

In a food processor fitted with the knife blade, blend the rosemary, oregano, and garlic until minced well. Season with salt and pepper. Set aside.

To prepare the chicken, preheat the oven to 450°F. Line 2 roasting pans with heavy-duty aluminum foil.

continued

In a large skillet over medium heat, heat the olive oil and sauté the onions, garlic, carrots, and zucchini until tender, about 5 minutes. Transfer the sautéed vegetables to the 2 prepared roasting pans.

Work the herb stuffing under the skin of the chicken pieces. Place the chicken on top of the vegetables. Arrange the rosemary and oregano sprigs on top. Season with salt and pepper. Pour wine and stock around the chicken and bake in the oven for 20 to 30 minutes until crisp on top and tender.

GLAZED GUINEA HENS

WHEN OUR children were young, I would cook a guinea hen for them when my husband and I went out for dinner. They would probably have been happy with hamburgers, but I wanted to give them a special treat.

Guinea hens are available at kosher butcher shops or in the freezer section of most supermarkets. These small game birds are a gourmet approach to poultry and make a welcome change from chicken and turkey.

MAKES 4 SERVINGS

Two 1½-pound guinea hens
Salt and freshly ground black pepper to taste
2 garlic cloves, minced
¼ cup orange or lemon marmalade
2 tablespoons extra-virgin olive oil

Preheat the oven to 500°F.

Line a large, shallow baking pan with heavy-duty aluminum foil (to save cleanup time) and place the guinea hens in the pan. Season the hens with salt and pepper.

In a small bowl, combine the garlic, marmalade, and olive oil. Brush the hens with the garlic mixture and bake about 15 minutes, then turn them and continue baking until bronze and cooked through, basting often with the remaining garlic mixture.

QUICK TURKEY CHILI

THIS CHILI is ready in only 30 minutes, but it is the kind of dish that improves when made 2 or 3 days ahead and reheated. I like to serve it with the traditional corn muffins, or with tortillas and Celeriac Slaw (page 54) or a refreshing Swedish Cucumber Salad (page 63).

MAKES 4 TO 6 SERVINGS

¼ cup extra-virgin olive oil

1 pound ground turkey

1 medium yellow onion, peeled and diced

3 cloves garlic, minced

1 large carrot, peeled and diced

1 celery stalk, diced

½ green bell pepper, diced

1 tablespoon chili powder

1 teaspoon cumin

One 16-ounce can whole tomatoes, chopped, with liquid

One 16-ounce can kidney or pinto beans, with liquid

1½ cups chopped cilantro leaves

Salt and freshly ground black pepper to taste

½ cup sliced scallions, for garnish

1 cup each chopped cilantro leaves, diced yellow onion, and diced green and red bell peppers, for garnish

Heat the olive oil in a large, deep pot over medium heat and brown the turkey, mixing and breaking into small pieces using a fork or wooden spoon, about 5 minutes. Add the onion, garlic, carrot, celery, green bell pepper, chili powder, and cumin, and sauté until the onion is translucent, about 5 minutes. Add the tomatoes and beans with their liquid and the cilantro. Bring to a boil and cover and simmer 20 minutes, or until flavors are well blended. Season with salt and pepper. Serve with bowls of scallions, cilantro, onion, and green and red bell peppers.

TURKEY KEBABS WITH HONEY GLAZE

ALITTLE TURKEY goes a long way in this quick and easy recipe. Serve the kebabs on a bed of quick-cooking rice, add a crisp salad, and you've got dinner in a matter of minutes.

MAKES 6 TO 8 SERVINGS

4 tablespoons honey
3 tablespoons balsamic or red wine vinegar
3 tablespoons extra-virgin olive oil
2 pounds boned, skinned turkey breast, cut into 1½-inch cubes
2 large red onions, peeled and cut into 12 wedges
2 large red bell peppers, cut into 12 wedges
Salt and freshly ground black pepper to taste
6–8 wooden or metal skewers, about 6 inches long

Preheat the oven to 400°F.

In a small bowl, combine the honey, vinegar, and 1 tablespoon of the olive oil.

Thread the turkey on wooden or metal skewers, alternating the turkey with the onion and red bell pepper wedges, and place in a large casserole dish. Pour the honey mixture over the turkey and season with salt and pepper. Marinate about 10 minutes.

Drain the marinade from the kebabs and reserve. Heat the remaining oil in a large ovenproof skillet over medium-high heat. When the oil is very hot, add the skewers and cook until the turkey is lightly browned on all sides, about 10 minutes. In a small saucepan, bring the marinade to a rolling boil, pour over the turkey, and bake until the turkey is cooked all the way through, about 10 minutes.

To serve, place the skewers on heated plates or remove the turkey and vegetables from the skewers and arrange on heated plates. Brush with saucepan drippings.

TURKEY SCHNITZEL

SCHNITZEL MEANS "cutlet," and this one is prepared with economical turkey instead of pricey veal. Turkey fillets are now sold in most kosher butcher shops. Buy a few extra and store them in your time-saver freezer.

MAKES 4 SERVINGS

8 slices (about 1 pound) thinly sliced turkey breast cutlets

2 egg whites

1 teaspoon water

2 tablespoons Dijon mustard

1¼ teaspoons salt

1 cup fine bread crumbs

½ teaspoon freshly ground black pepper

6 tablespoons extra-virgin olive oil

Pound the turkey cutlets lightly with a mallet or a frying pan between 2 pieces of waxed paper.

In a medium bowl, beat the egg whites with the water. Mix in the mustard and ½ teaspoon of the salt. In a shallow dish, mix the bread crumbs with the remaining ¾ teaspoon salt and pepper. Set aside. Dip each cutlet in the egg white mixture, then coat both sides with bread crumbs.

In a large nonstick skillet, heat 3 tablespoons of the olive oil over medium heat. Add half the cutlets and cook, turning once, until golden brown and cooked through, 2 to 3 minutes per side. Transfer to paper towels and drain. Wipe out the skillet and cook the remaining cutlets in the remaining 3 tablespoons oil.

ZIPLOC CHICKEN SURPRISE

ZIPLOC BAGS offer a great new way to cook! Chef Michel Richard of Citrus restaurant, in Los Angeles, shared this invaluable cooking tip with me when he appeared on my television show. Poached in the airtight freezer bag, the bird cooks quickly but remains moist and succulent.

MAKES 4 SERVINGS

One 3-pound fryer chicken
Salt and freshly ground black pepper to taste
1 tablespoon Pareve Chicken Stock (page 33)
1 cup Concord grape wine or port wine, heated
1 medium zucchini, cut into ½-inch dice
1 large crookneck squash, cut into ½-inch dice
5–6 mushrooms, cut into ½-inch dice
1 leek, white part only, cut into ½-inch dice

Season the chicken with salt and pepper and place in a large Ziploc plastic freezer bag. Dissolve the powdered stock in the wine and add to the chicken. Add the zucchini, squash, mushrooms, and leek. Remove the air from the bag and zip it closed. Place it in a large pot filled with gently simmering, but not boiling, water for 25 minutes, or until tender.

To serve, open the bag and pour the broth into a large bowl. Remove the chicken from the bag using tongs and carve it into individual serving pieces. Remove the vegetables from the bag and spoon into individual serving plates. Place the chicken on top of the vegetables and spoon some broth over them.

CHICKEN BREASTS IN PACKAGES

IT's **FUN** to serve guests their main course in a gift-wrapped package. When chicken breasts and vegetables are wrapped and cooked in aluminum foil, they release the most fragrant aroma when the packages are opened tableside.

MAKES 8 SERVINGS

Eight 8-ounce chicken breasts, skinned and boned
4 scallions, julienned
4 carrots, peeled and julienned
2 parsnips, peeled and julienned
2 slices fresh ginger, peeled and julienned
8 fresh rosemary sprigs
½ cup unsalted nondairy margarine
Salt and freshly ground black pepper to taste

Preheat the oven to 500°F.

Tear off 8 sheets of foil, 11 × 12 inches each. Place a chicken breast over the center of the lower half of each sheet, skin side up. Arrange an equal amount of scallions, carrots, parsnips, ginger, and rosemary over each chicken breast. Dot each breast with margarine. Season with salt and pepper. Seal the packages by crimping the edges of the foil securely to make airtight envelopes. (You can refrigerate the packages at this point for 2 to 3 hours.)

Place a foil-lined baking sheet in the oven for 5 minutes. Arrange the chicken packages on the baking sheet in a single layer. Bake for 10 to 15 minutes, or until the breasts are done and the juices run clear. (Open a fold of one package and test the chicken with a fork for doneness; the fork should pierce through the chicken easily.)

To serve, place each "surprise" package on serving plates and let guests open their own. Or carefully open the envelopes and, using a metal spatula, transfer the chicken and vegetables to serving plates, and spoon the sauce from the package over the chicken. Serve immediately.

GRANDMA'S PICKLED CHICKEN

THE **FRENCH** use a lot of vinegar when cooking chicken; they know it makes the poultry moist and tender. Try serving this dish cold for a summer buffet, as a novel substitute for gefilte fish.

A bouquet garni is a combination of herbs, usually wrapped in cheesecloth. I like to wrap the herbs in leek leaves; they add flavor besides providing a holder for the herbs.

MAKES 4 SERVINGS

1 Bouquet Garni (recipe follows)
⅓ cup extra-virgin olive oil
One 1½- to 2-pound chicken, cut into 8 serving pieces
¾ cup dry white wine
¾ cup distilled white vinegar
¾ cup hot water
1 medium yellow onion, peeled and cut into ⅛-inch wedges
2 carrots, peeled and thinly sliced into rounds
1 small leek, including 2 inches of the green part, thinly sliced
1 teaspoon salt
Lemon slices, for garnish

Prepare the Bouquet Garni.

In a large, heavy pot, heat the olive oil over medium-high heat, and brown the chicken, skin side down, turning once, about 5 minutes.

Add the wine, vinegar, water, onion, carrots, leek, salt, and Bouquet Garni, and bring to a boil over high heat. Reduce the heat to low, cover and simmer for 25 minutes, or until the chicken is tender but not falling apart.

Remove the Bouquet Garni and arrange the chicken pieces in an 8 × 10-inch deep baking dish, just large enough to hold them snugly in one layer. Pour the cooking liquid with the vegetables over the chicken. Cool to room temperature, about 15 minutes. Cover with plastic wrap and refrigerate. Serve when cold garnished with lemon slices.

continued

BOUQUET GARNI

2 outer green leaves from 1 large leek

1 celery top

2 parsley sprigs

2 bay leaves

2 whole cloves

¼ teaspoon dried thyme

Place 1 leek leaf on the work surface and flatten by pressing with the palm of your hand. Arrange the celery top, parsley, bay leaves, cloves, and thyme in the center. Cover with the remaining leek leaf and tie with string to make a tight bundle. Set aside.

CHICKEN JAMBALAYA

A FAMOUS JEWISH comedian once said that Purim was his favorite holiday because it reminded him of Mardi Gras. "Purim has everything," he said, "singing, dancing, masquerades, and the opportunity to drink lots of wine." His remarks inspired me to create this dish to serve at our Purim dinner.

MAKES 6 SERVINGS

2 whole bay leaves, minced or ground

1 teaspoon dried thyme

¼ teaspoon dried sage

½ teaspoon cayenne pepper or to taste

1½ teaspoons salt

½ teaspoons freshly ground black pepper

2 tablespoons extra-virgin olive oil

6 boneless, skinless chicken breast halves, cut into 1-inch chunks

3 garlic cloves, minced

1 large yellow onion, peeled and diced

3 celery stalks, thinly sliced

1 large green bell pepper, diced

1 cup fresh or frozen okra, ends trimmed, and cut into thirds

One 14½-ounce can peeled, diced tomatoes

One 8-ounce can tomato sauce

2½ cups Chicken Stock (page 32)

1½ cups uncooked long-grain rice

In a small bowl, combine the bay leaves, thyme, sage, cayenne pepper, and salt and pepper. Set aside.

In a 2-quart saucepan over high heat, heat the olive oil. Add the chicken and sauté until browned, about 5 minutes, turning frequently. Stir in the bay leaf mixture, garlic, onion, celery, and green bell pepper. Cook until vegetables are tender, about 5 minutes, stirring occasionally.

Stir in the okra, tomatoes (with juice), tomato sauce, stock, and rice, mixing well. Bring to a boil. Simmer, covered, 20 minutes, stirring every 5 to 10 minutes until rice is tender. To serve, ladle into heated, shallow bowls.

MINCED CHICKEN IN LETTUCE WRAPPERS

IN MOST Chinese restaurants, this popular dish is usually made with squab. Made with chicken, it's easy to prepare and fun to serve as finger food. The lettuce leaves replace bread to make the "sandwich," so you may roll the minced chicken in the lettuce leaves and serve. Or pass the chicken mixture and lettuce leaves in separate bowls and let guests fill and roll their own.

MAKES 4 SERVINGS

Hoisin Sauce (recipe follows)
2 whole chicken breasts (about 16 ounces), boned, skinned, and cut into ¼-inch dice
1 teaspoon sugar
4 teaspoons cornstarch
1 tablespoon soy sauce
2 tablespoons sherry
3 teaspoons minced garlic
Freshly ground black pepper to taste
3 tablespoons vegetable oil
4 scallions, thinly sliced (white and green parts)
5 mushrooms, chopped
One 8-ounce can bamboo shoots, diced (optional)
⅔ cup Chicken Stock (page 32)
1 teaspoon cornstarch
1 head iceberg lettuce, leaves separated

Prepare the Hoisin Sauce and refrigerate.

Mix the chicken with the sugar, cornstarch, soy sauce, sherry, 1 teaspoon of the minced garlic, and pepper.

In a wok, heat the oil over medium-high heat and add the remaining minced garlic and scallions; sauté for 1 minute. Add the mushrooms, and if using, bamboo shoots, and stir-fry on high heat for 2 minutes, or until liquid is evaporated, stirring frequently. Add the chicken mixture and cook about 2 minutes, or until chicken is cooked through. Add the stock and cornstarch, and cook 1 minute.

Spread 1 teaspoon of Hoisin Sauce on each lettuce leaf. Place some of the chicken mixture in the center of each leaf. Fold the ends and sides of the lettuce leaves over the filling and roll up. Arrange on serving plates.

HOISIN SAUCE

MAKES ABOUT ⅓ CUP

4 tablespoons hoisin-type sauce
2 tablespoons cold water
1 teaspoon sugar
2 teaspoons sesame oil

In a small bowl, combine the hoisin sauce, water, sugar, and sesame oil; mix well. Cover with plastic wrap and refrigerate, up to 2 or 3 days.

CREOLE CHICKEN

SAVOR NEW ORLEANS flavors in minutes. To save time, brown the chicken while the sauce is simmering. You can serve this robust dish with rice or noodles. I think kasha is a perfect choice.

MAKES 4 SERVINGS

½ cup extra-virgin olive oil
1 large yellow onion, peeled and chopped
1 medium green bell pepper, chopped
2 garlic cloves, minced
One 2-pound can whole tomatoes, with juice, diced
1 bay leaf
1 teaspoon salt
8 whole peppercorns
½ teaspoon paprika
1 tablespoon brown sugar
2 tablespoons golden raisins
½ cup dry red wine
One 3-pound frying chicken, cut into 8 pieces
Salt and freshly ground black pepper to taste

In a large skillet, heat ¼ cup of the oil over medium-high heat and sauté the onion, green bell pepper, and garlic until tender, 2 minutes. Add the tomatoes, with the juice, bay leaf, salt, peppercorns, and paprika; bring to a boil over high heat, reduce the heat to medium, and simmer, about 5 minutes. Add the brown sugar, raisins, and wine; increase the heat and bring to a boil.

Preheat the oven to 400°F.

Season the chicken with salt and pepper and sauté in a large skillet in the remaining oil over medium-high heat, on both sides, for 5 minutes. Transfer the chicken, skin side up, in a single layer to a roasting pan and pour the sauce over the chicken. Bake until the chicken is tender, about 20 minutes.

To serve, arrange the chicken and sauce on individual serving plates with kasha.

COLD ROASTED CHICKEN WITH FENNEL AND LEEKS

CARRIE **N**AHABEDIAN, the chef at the Four Seasons Hotel in Los Angeles, prepared this elegant dish for one thousand guests, at a gala celebrating the Fiftieth Anniversary of the State of Israel during the week of Passover. Of necessity, Carrie served the chicken cold, but it is equally moist and delicate served hot, right from the oven.

MAKES 4 SERVINGS

Janie Masters' Red Wine Sauce (recipe follows)
2 tablespoons extra-virgin olive oil
1 medium fennel bulb, finely diced (about 2 cups)
2 medium leeks, cleaned and finely diced (about 3 cups)
½ cup chopped chives
8 garlic cloves, minced
Salt and freshly ground black pepper to taste
2 whole boneless chicken breasts, 8 ounces each, skin on, cut in half
Extra-virgin olive oil, for brushing chicken and baking pan

Prepare Janie Masters' Red Wine Sauce.

Preheat the oven to 425°F.

In a heavy-bottomed saucepan, heat the olive oil over medium-high heat, and sauté the fennel, leeks, chives, and garlic until soft, about 10 minutes. Season with salt and pepper. Cool.

Place the chicken breasts on a cutting board, skin side down. With a sharp knife trim off excess fat and skin. Pound each chicken breast lightly between 2 sheets of plastic wrap with a meat pounder or heavy pot to an even thickness.

Place 1 chicken breast on a cutting board, skin side down; season with salt and pepper, take a heaping tablespoon of the fennel mixture and mold it into a cigar shape, and place it in the center of the chicken breast. Roll the chicken breast around the stuffing, tie with string, and brush with oil. Place on a foil-lined baking pan that has been brushed with oil. Repeat with the remaining chicken breasts.

continued

Bake until the chicken is browned and firm to the touch, about 20 minutes. Transfer to a cutting board, remove the string, and slice on the bias.

To serve, arrange the sliced chicken on serving plates and spoon the sauce on the side.

JANIE MASTERS' RED WINE SAUCE

THIS RICH wine sauce complements chicken as well as turkey, lamb, or a simple hamburger. Janie Masters, an English friend living in the south of France, is a fabulous chef and restaurant owner. She prepares this sauce using the wines from their vineyard. Janie calls it the essence of wine and serves it with lamb.

MAKES ½ CUP

1 bottle dry red wine
4 tablespoons red currant or grape jelly
1 teaspoon sugar
Peel of 1 pear or apple
Peels of 1 lemon and 1 orange

In a large, heavy pot, combine the wine, jelly, sugar, and peels. Bring to a boil over high heat and boil until reduced to ½ cup, about 30 minutes. Remove peels.

CHAPTER NINE

*

MEAT

WHEN I was growing up, a rib-eye steak, canned peas, and a baked potato were considered a special meal. After I married my husband, Marvin, I realized that I wanted to expand my options under the category of special meals. So, Marvin and I began experimenting with different cuts of beef, lamb, and veal.

As I mentioned in the Introduction, I used to think brisket and pot roast were the easiest way to cook a meat-based meal. Just like my grandmother and mother before me, I'd toss a lot of vegetables in with the beef, add some tomato sauce and red wine or water, and then let it all cook for hours.

I know why I made slow-roasted beef so often; it was simple and it was always successful. I think that's why everyone turns to braised beef or a quickly broiled steak. You don't need a recipe and you can't mess it up. In actuality, there are many fast and easy ways to prepare meat that are certainly more healthful.

Most kosher meats require long cooking times, so I haven't included many meat recipes in this book. Besides, I most often cook with fish, poultry, grains, pastas, and vegetables. But the meat recipes that are in this chapter are great. Liver and Onions is an all-time classic, and my recipe delivers the traditional great taste. Stuffed Hamburgers, filled with a salsalike vegetable mixture, are fun to make and can even become a family project. If you crave a simple yet sophisticated meat course, turn to Skillet-Grilled Lamb Chops. You'll be amazed how easy it is to prepare this dish and how the balsamic vinegar really makes the chops sparkle.

MEAT

— * —

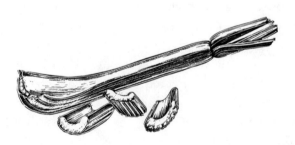

A SIMPLE GUIDE TO KOSHER MEAT

Surprisingly, the definition of what is kosher, and what is not, is not as clear-cut as you may think. The confusion is mainly due to the fact that different names are given to some cuts of meat. I have tried to use only generic names, such as lamb chop. Beware of names that look the same, such as flanken, which is kosher, and flank steak, which is not.

After doing a lot of research and interviewing a number of kosher butchers (and buying a lot of meat), I have arrived at these guidelines. If you have any questions, talk to your butcher; I am sure he can supply you with all the kosher cuts of beef, lamb, and veal I have indicated in the recipes in this book.

Kosher cuts of beef, from forequarters: beef cheek, breast flanken, rib flanken, brisket, chuck (used for ground meat, fillet steak, or pot roast), rib top, rib eye, rib steak, boned rib steak, short rib, shoulder roast, shoulder steak, skirt steak, standing rib roast, and beef tongue.

Kosher cuts of veal, from forequarters: veal breast, brisket, cutlets, ribs (chops), shoulder, shoulder steak, and veal tongue.

Kosher cuts of lamb, from forequarters: breast brisket, neck, rib, shank, shoulder lamb chops, and lamb tongue.

LIVER AND ONIONS

PREPARED PROPERLY, liver can taste rich and almost velvety. And when sautéed with onions, it truly transcends the ordinary.

To save time in preparing and serving this dish, sauté the onions in advance, and just season and cook the liver at the last minute.

MAKES 4 SERVINGS

4 tablespoons extra-virgin olive oil
3 cups thinly sliced yellow onions
Salt and freshly ground black pepper to taste
1½ pounds calf's liver (see Note), trimmed and cut into ¼-inch slices
1 teaspoon minced fresh sage or ½ teaspoon dried sage
1 tablespoon dry white wine
1½ tablespoons white wine vinegar

Heat the oil in a large, heavy skillet over medium heat. Add the onions, season with salt and pepper, and cook over low heat, stirring frequently, until golden and very tender, about 10 minutes.

Transfer the onions to a bowl, leaving the oil in the skillet.

Increase the heat to high and add the liver, tossing it in the oil for about 3 minutes until the liver begins to brown. Sprinkle with the sage, wine, vinegar, salt, and pepper, and reduce the heat to low.

Return the onions to the pan, just to reheat them, and serve with the liver and pan juices at once.

NOTE: *Prepared according to kosher dietary laws.*

STUFFED HAMBURGER "SWINGERS"

MANY YEARS ago there was a health food restaurant on Hollywood's famed Sunset Strip named The Aware Inn. It was the first to make hamburgers, called "Swingers," stuffed with a mix of onions, tomatoes, and green peppers—almost a salsa except it was sandwiched between the meat. They tasted so good, we have been preparing hamburgers this way ever since.

MAKES 4 SERVINGS

1 garlic clove, minced
¼ cup yellow onion, peeled and finely diced
¼ cup tomato, finely diced
¼ cup green bell pepper, finely diced
1 teaspoon dried oregano
Salt and freshly ground black pepper to taste
1 pound lean ground beef
1 egg
3 tablespoons extra-virgin olive oil
2 large yellow onions, peeled and thinly sliced

In a medium bowl, combine the garlic, diced onion, tomato, green bell pepper, and oregano. Add the salt and pepper, and mix well. Cover with plastic wrap and set aside.

In a large bowl, combine the ground beef, egg, salt, and pepper. Shape into eight 4-inch round, flat patties. Place a spoonful of the vegetable filling in the center of one patty, top with a second patty, press down firmly, and shape into a round, carefully sealing the sides by pinching together. Repeat with the remaining patties.

In a large nonstick skillet, heat the oil over medium-high heat and sauté the sliced onions until lightly brown. Transfer to a bowl and keep warm. Brown the hamburgers for about 5 minutes on each side, or until cooked to medium; return the onions to the pan and heat. Serve immediately.

SAUTÉED VEAL BURGERS

VEAL IS leaner than beef, and sautéed veal burgers provide an easy, effective alternative to more mundane ground beef dishes. Simple accompaniments such as fried onions, grilled mushrooms, steamed vegetables, or mashed potatoes complement these burgers perfectly. Or serve veal patties on toasted sesame seed buns, topped with roasted peppers.

MAKES 6 SERVINGS

> 6 tablespoons extra-virgin olive oil
> 3 shallots, minced
> 1 pound ground veal
> ¼ cup packaged bread crumbs
> Pinch of grated nutmeg
> 1 teaspoon dried thyme
> 2 tablespoons minced fresh parsley
> 2 tablespoons cold water
> ¼ teaspoon salt
> ¼ teaspoon freshly ground black pepper
> ½ cup unbleached all-purpose flour

In a skillet over medium heat, heat 3 tablespoons of the olive oil and sauté the shallots until softened, about 2 minutes.

In a large mixing bowl, combine the shallots, veal, bread crumbs, nutmeg, thyme, parsley, water, salt, and pepper. Mix lightly but thoroughly.

Divide the veal mixture into 6 equal portions and shape into patties. In a non-stick skillet over medium heat, heat the remaining oil. Lightly dust the patties with flour. Sauté about 4 minutes per side, or until well browned.

To serve, arrange on heated plates with a hamburger bun, mustard, sliced tomatoes, and salad greens.

SKILLET-GRILLED LAMB CHOPS WITH MUSHROOM SAUCE

IT TAKES only minutes to grill thick lamb chops to perfection. I like to use first-cut chops; they're small but thick and are preferable to very large chops, as they're more tender and they cook faster.

Daryl Corti, my Sacramento foodie friend, once served us grilled lamb chops with fifty-year-old balsamic vinegar at a dinner he prepared for us.

MAKES 4 SERVINGS

2 tablespoons extra-virgin olive oil
2 cups small shiitake mushrooms, cut into ½-inch dice
1 cup Chicken Stock (page 32)
¼ cup fresh rosemary leaves, chopped
Salt and freshly ground black pepper to taste
8 first-cut lamb chops, 1½ inches thick
Balsamic vinegar

In a nonstick skillet over medium heat, heat the olive oil and sauté the mushrooms for 5 minutes until soft. Add the chicken stock and cook over high heat until reduced by half. Keep warm.

Sprinkle rosemary, salt, and pepper on both sides of the lamb chops. Sprinkle salt into a heavy, ridged, iron skillet, and on high heat, heat the skillet until it is very hot. Place the lamb chops in the skillet, or on the grill, and cook for 5 minutes until brown on the bottom. Turn and cook the chops for about 3 minutes more until medium rare (pink in the center).

To serve, arrange the lamb chops on heated serving plates and spoon the mushroom sauce on top. Serve balsamic vinegar on the side. Serve with Vegetable Couscous (page 103) or Brown Rice with Honeyed Apples (page 100).

SWEET AND HOT LAMB WITH PLUM GLAZE

EVERYBODY WILL think you spent hours preparing this spicy lamb with its Asian accents of soy, ginger, and hot red pepper. In actuality, it takes only 25 minutes to prepare. To save time, cook the sauce in advance and refrigerate it until ready to use.

MAKES 4 SERVINGS

One 16-ounce can purple plums with syrup
½ teaspoon crushed red pepper flakes or to taste
2 tablespoons honey
2 tablespoons distilled white vinegar
2 tablespoons soy sauce
2 garlic cloves, minced
1 teaspoon peeled and minced fresh ginger
2½–3 pounds lamb shoulder, trimmed of all fat, cut in 1½-inch cubes
8 wooden or metal skewers, 6 inches long

Preheat the broiler or grill.

Drain the plums and discard the pits. Reserve the syrup and set aside.

In a food processor or blender, puree the plums and transfer to a medium saucepan. Add the red pepper flakes, honey, vinegar, soy sauce, garlic, and ginger. Mix well and bring to a boil over high heat. Reduce the heat to low and simmer for 15 minutes, stirring occasionally. Stir in ¾ to 1 cup of the reserved syrup, just enough to keep the sauce from becoming too thick. Thread the lamb onto the skewers and broil or grill, about 5 minutes per side, basting with the sauce.

Bring the remaining sauce to a boil, transfer to a bowl, and serve for dipping. Serve the lamb.

OVEN-BRAISED LAMB IN FOIL

ALAMB SHOULDER roast would take at least 1½ hours to bake, but you can save time by cutting the lamb in small chunks. The aroma and flavor are wonderful, and there is no mess to clean up. Add some tiny steamed potatoes to the package and you have a one-dish meal.

MAKES 6 SERVINGS

2 pounds lamb shoulder, cut in 2-inch chunks, fat removed
2 garlic cloves, sliced
Salt and freshly ground black pepper to taste
2 bay leaves, crushed
½ cup chopped fresh parsley
¼ cup minced fresh tarragon
Grated zest of 1 lemon
Juice of 1 lemon

Preheat the oven to 400°F.

Spread the lamb chunks out on a large piece of double-strength aluminum foil; sprinkle with the garlic, salt, pepper, bay leaves, parsley, tarragon, and lemon zest. Pour the lemon juice over the lamb. Fold the sides of the foil over the lamb, and seal tightly. Place on a baking pan. Bake for 30 minutes until the lamb is tender.

COOKING WITH FOIL

Sometimes when you're baking it's fun to be lazy and wrap everything in foil. Then you can forget about basting and turning the food. For this quick-and-easy meal, every component is encased in the foil. When it's unwrapped, all you have to do is serve it.

Be sure to season the food well before baking, and add your favorite vegetables, such as potatoes, onions, mushrooms, and zucchini.

SKIRT STEAK "LOLLIPOPS"

T AKE ADVANTAGE of this money-saving cut of meat by being your own butcher. Pound the steak; roll it, cut it, and marinate it; then broil it and it's ready to serve. No one will ever notice that it's not as tasty and tender as pricey filet mignon, which isn't kosher, anyway. For a special occasion, serve the steak with Janie Masters' Red Wine Sauce (page 138) and Kathy's Green Beans (page 75).

MAKES 4 TO 8 SERVINGS

Marinade (below)
Two 24-inch-long strips (about 2 pounds) skirt steak
Wooden skewers (soaked in water)

Prepare the Marinade.

Place skirt steaks on a work surface and cut each in half, making four 12-inch strips. Starting at the narrow end, roll each one lengthwise as tight as possible, jelly-roll style. Push 2 skewers through each roll, about 2 inches apart, to fasten. With a sharp knife, slice in half, so you have 2 rolled "lollipop" steaks. Set aside.

In a large, shallow baking dish, pour in the Marinade, arrange the lollipop steaks in the marinade, and marinate at room temperature for 10 minutes, turning to coat both sides.

Heat the broiler; place the "lollipop" steaks on a foil-lined broiler pan and broil, turning once, about 5 minutes each side for rare on the inside and brown and crisp on the exterior.

MARINADE

MAKES ABOUT 1¼ CUPS

½ cup soy sauce
½ cup dry red wine
2 tablespoons extra-virgin olive oil
3 garlic cloves, minced
One 1-inch piece fresh ginger, peeled and minced

In a large, shallow glass bowl, combine the soy sauce, red wine, olive oil, garlic, and ginger; mix well. Cover with plastic wrap and refrigerate until ready to use.

STIR-FRY LONDON BROIL

WITH JUST a few ingredients and a few minutes, you can create a stir-fry dish for dinner tonight. This particular recipe was inspired by the vegetables and condiments we found in the refrigerator one day.

The meat was frozen, so we defrosted it slightly before slicing it. It's best to have the meat partially frozen to obtain the thinnest possible slices.

MAKES 4 SERVINGS

½ pound London broil

¼ cup extra-virgin olive oil

3 garlic cloves, minced

3 teaspoons peeled and minced fresh ginger

8 scallions, sliced on the diagonal into ½-inch pieces

1 pound (about 20 leaves) Swiss chard, ½ inch wide, shredded

1 cup Chicken Stock (page 32)

2 teaspoons sesame oil

4 tablespoons soy sauce

2 tablespoons sugar

Slice the steak on the diagonal as thinly as possible. Set aside.

In a medium skillet, over high heat, heat the olive oil and add the garlic, ginger, and scallions, stirring for 1 minute. Add the chard and cook for 2 minutes, then add ½ cup of the stock, and stir until chard is wilted, about 3 minutes. Transfer the mixture to a bowl.

In a wok, over high heat, heat the remaining stock and sesame oil, add the meat, soy sauce, and sugar, and cook, tossing to brown the meat evenly. Add the reserved chard mixture and toss until heated through, about 3 minutes. Serve with white or brown rice.

VARIATION: *Substitute other vegetables in this stir-fry, such as mushrooms, broccoli, green bell peppers, and savoy cabbage.*

MOLLY'S GLAZED MEAT LOAF

HERE'S A quick-cooking meat loaf with some old-fashioned ingredients, hard-boiled eggs in the center, and a catsup glaze on top. Serve it with homey side dishes like Gerri Gilliland's Colcannon (page 69) or Holiday Sweet Potato Kugel (page 180). The meat loaf makes a great sandwich with slices of Classic Challah (page 175) and mustard.

MAKES 8 SERVINGS

4 small hard-boiled eggs (page 58), peeled

2 pounds ground beef

2 eggs

1 cup dried bread crumbs

½ medium onion, peeled and grated

2 garlic cloves, minced

1 cup catsup

Salt and freshly ground black pepper to taste

1½ cups dry red wine

3 large onions, peeled and thinly sliced

Prepare the hard-boiled eggs and refrigerate.

In a large bowl, combine the beef, eggs, bread crumbs, grated onion, garlic, and 2 tablespoons of the catsup, salt and pepper, and ¼ cup of the red wine; mix well.

Preheat the oven to 425°F.

In a large roaster, arrange the sliced onions. Shape half of the meat mixture into a flat loaf and place it on top of the onions in the roaster. Place the hard-boiled eggs lengthwise along the center of the molded meat loaf. Mold the remaining meat mixture on top of the eggs, gently pressing to form a loaf.

In a small bowl, blend 4 tablespoons catsup and the remaining 1¼ cups wine. Pour the wine mixture around the entire loaf. Spread the remaining catsup on top of the meat loaf as you would frost a cake. Cover and bake for 30 minutes until baked through. Remove from the oven and let rest in the covered roaster until ready to serve.

CHAPTER TEN

✳

DESSERTS

I confess. I have quite a sweet tooth and have claimed one since I was seven years old. When my friends were playing with dolls, I was playing with dough—chocolate chip cookie dough, to be exact. Two years later, I was mimicking my aunt Betty in the kitchen, baking cinnamon rolls and preparing her sour cream coffee cake under her watchful eye.

My propensity for baking certainly made me a popular teenager. Many of my classmates liked to stop by after school to sample my latest creations. As I grew older, I found that my boyfriends were quite taken with the apple and lemon meringue pies I could whip up with ease. One of those boyfriends was named Marvin Zeidler and, yes, he became my husband. And while I still can make a mean lemon meringue pie, I often tempt Marvin with other desserts, many of which are in this book.

These sweets may look like a million dollars, but they take only minutes to prepare. I premeasure all the ingredients so that when it comes time to bake, the preparation time is kept to a minimum.

For a light, refreshing dessert, try Strawberries with Raspberry Sauce or Coconut Sorbet. Banana "Brownie" Bars sound wicked, but they contain healthful ingredients like whole wheat flour and bananas.

The Apple Pizza is one of my favorites. I like to serve this hot-from-the-oven dessert for Rosh Hashanah. It's a wonderful way to ring in the Jewish New

Year! Individual Ricotta Soufflés make a great dinner finale when you are entertaining guests. And if just the mention of old-fashioned sour cream coffee cake makes you sigh with delight, you will be thrilled with the Cinnamon-Buttermilk Coffee Cake, for which I created a special technique to reduce the preparation time.

When serving these desserts, remember to substitute nondairy margarine and nondairy creamer if you're serving a meat-based meal, since kosher dietary rules forbid the mixing of meat and dairy food at the same meal.

Now go bake and enjoy!

BUTTER AND NONDAIRY MARGARINE

I never use *salted* butter or *salted* margarine when cooking or baking. Salt causes a change in flavor. With unsalted butter you get the pure butter taste, which is fresh and slightly sweet. To keep unsalted butter or margarine, store in the freezer until you're ready to use it. In almost all of my kosher cooking and baking, butter and nondairy margarine are interchangeable—keeping in mind the kosher dietary laws, of course.

DESSERTS

BUTTER AND NONDAIRY MARGARINE

APPLE PIZZA

CINNAMON-BUTTERMILK COFFEE CAKE

BANANA "BROWNIE" BARS

MEASURING FLOUR

LACY ALMOND CUPS

PICCOLI SOUFFLÉS DI RICOTTA (INDIVIDUAL RICOTTA SOUFFLÉS)

SOUFFLÉS

CELESTINO DRAGO'S TIRAMISÙ

STRAWBERRIES WITH RASPBERRY SAUCE

JOAN BRAM'S TRIPLE CHOCOLATE COOKIES

PURIM SEED CRISPS

FRENCH TOAST "SANDWICH" SURPRISE

QUEEN ESTHER'S TOAST

POTATO WAFFLE LATKES

COCONUT SORBET

CHOCOLATE CHIP COCONUT SORBET

POPPY SEED HAMANTASCHEN (PAGE 182)

PASSOVER HAZELNUT SPONGE CAKE (PAGE 187)

APPLE PIZZA

HONEY AND apples make this simply delicious pizza a perfect dessert to serve at the Jewish New Year. Hot from the oven, this unusual dessert or brunch treat is bound to please the entire family.

Just prepare the Quick Basic Pizza Dough, roll it out, cover it with applesauce, apple slices, and apricot glaze, bake in a hot oven, and in less than 30 minutes, you can say, "Dessert is served."

MAKES 4 (12-INCH) PIZZAS, ABOUT 16 SERVINGS

⅓ cup extra-virgin olive oil
1 recipe Quick Basic Pizza Dough (page 11)
½ cup Apricot Glaze (recipe follows)
4 Golden Delicious apples
One 8-ounce jar applesauce
1 egg yolk, lightly beaten

Preheat the oven to 400°F. Brush a pizza pan or baking sheet with 1 tablespoon of the oil.

Prepare the Quick Basic Pizza Dough and the Apricot Glaze, and set aside.

Divide the dough into 4 pieces. Working with 1 piece at a time, roll it out and slip it onto the prepared pan. Brush the dough with oil.

Cut the apples in half, core, and cut them into thin slices. Spread one fourth of the applesauce over each dough round and arrange one fourth of the apple slices on top. Beginning in the middle of the pizza, form a spiral of the apple slices, covering as much of the applesauce as you can.

Quickly brush a generous amount of glaze over the apples so they will not discolor.

Brush the yolk onto the exposed edges of the crust. Bake the pizza in the preheated oven for about 20 minutes, or until the crust is golden brown. After 15 minutes, check the pizza to be sure the crust is not overbrowning. Repeat with the remaining 3 pieces of dough, applesauce, and apples.

NOTE: *For 12 small pizzas, divide the dough into 12 pieces, roll out, and proceed as directed above.*

APRICOT GLAZE

MAKES ABOUT ½ CUP

¼ *cup nondairy margarine*
¼ *cup apricot jam*

Melt the margarine in a small pan over low heat with the apricot jam and stir to blend.

CINNAMON-BUTTERMILK COFFEE CAKE

I **ADAPTED THIS** rustic coffee cake from a favorite family recipe. I had always disliked preparing a separate streusel topping, so by adding nuts to some of the batter and setting it aside, I created an instant one. Bake this cake in a shallow baking pan instead of a Bundt pan—it's faster yet the cake is just as delicious.

MAKES 12 SERVINGS

¾ cup plus 2 tablespoons vegetable oil
1½ cups almonds (½ cup ground and 1 cup sliced)
2¼ cups unbleached all-purpose flour
1 cup brown sugar, packed
¾ cup granulated sugar
2 teaspoons ground cinnamon
½ teaspoon salt
¼ teaspoon ground ginger
1 teaspoon baking powder
1 teaspoon baking soda
1 large egg
1 cup buttermilk

Preheat the oven to 350°F. Brush a 13 × 9-inch baking dish with 2 tablespoons of the oil and sprinkle with ground almonds.

In a medium bowl, mix the flour, sugars, 1 teaspoon of the cinnamon, salt, and ginger. Blend in the remaining oil until smooth. Remove ¾ cup of the flour mixture and combine with the slivered almonds and remaining 1 teaspoon cinnamon. Mix well and set aside. (This mixture becomes the streusel topping.)

To the remaining flour mixture, add the baking powder, baking soda, egg, and buttermilk. Blend until smooth. Pour into the prepared baking pan. Sprinkle the reserved streusel mixture evenly over the surface of the batter. Bake for 25 minutes, or until a toothpick inserted in the center of the cake comes out clean. Cool the cake in the pan on a wire rack. Cut into 12 squares.

NOTE: *Purchase unpeeled, sliced almonds and grind the quantity needed for the recipe in a food processor or blender.*

BANANA "BROWNIE" BARS

THESE EASY-to-prepare bars combine the natural sweetness of bananas and raisins with the heartiness of whole wheat flour and cornmeal. Poppy seeds add a distinctive flavor and crunch. The bars are so delicious you will want to double the recipe and freeze some.

MAKES 16 BARS

½ cup unsalted butter or nondairy margarine
⅔ cup brown sugar, packed
1 large egg
1 teaspoon vanilla
1½ cups mashed ripe bananas
1¼ cups unbleached all-purpose flour
½ cup whole wheat flour
¼ cup cornmeal
2 tablespoons cocoa
2 teaspoons baking powder
½ teaspoon salt
2 tablespoons poppy seeds
¾ cup toasted, coarsely chopped walnuts (page 101)
½ cup finely ground walnuts (optional)
Chocolate Glaze or Sauce (recipe follows)

Preheat the oven to 350°F.

In the bowl of an electric mixer, cream the butter or margarine and brown sugar. Add the egg, vanilla, and bananas, mixing well.

In another bowl, combine the two flours, cornmeal, cocoa, baking powder, salt, and poppy seeds. Stir into the butter mixture, mixing just to blend. Stir in the coarsely chopped walnuts.

Brush a 13 × 9-inch baking pan with butter or margarine and dust with ground walnuts, if using. Bake in the oven for 20 to 25 minutes, or until the edges are golden brown and the cake pulls away from the sides of the pan. Cool in the pan on a wire rack. Spread the Chocolate Glaze evenly on top of the brownie bars. Cut into 16 rectangles.

CHOCOLATE GLAZE OR SAUCE

MAKES ABOUT 1 CUP

8 ounces semisweet chocolate, coarsely chopped
½ cup strong hot coffee
½ cup apricot or strawberry preserves, strained
1 tablespoon fruit liqueur, optional

In the top of a double boiler over simmering water (or in a microwave), melt the chocolate, coffee, preserves, and liqueur, if using. With a wooden spoon, mix constantly until the mixture is melted and well blended. Transfer to a glass bowl, cover with plastic wrap, and refrigerate. Serve hot or cold.

MEASURING FLOUR

When baking, it is crucial to measure flour, as well as sugar, accurately. I sift flour only when making a sponge cake or if specified in a recipe. When you're baking cakes, cookies, or breads—the most accurate way to measure the flour is to spoon it into a measuring cup and level the top with a straight-edge, such as the handle of a spatula or the side of a knife. Never tap the measuring cup on the counter. The flour will settle, and if you add more flour to fill the measuring cup, it will make the pastry too heavy.

LACY ALMOND CUPS

THIS IS one of the first fancy desserts I made as a young bride. I was so proud that I could make something so delicate and pretty. The ingredients, which are basic, just take a few minutes to mix together. Just scoop your favorite ice cream into the crisp cups and drizzle with chocolate sauce or combine small scoops of Coconut Sorbet (page 170) with fresh berries.

MAKES 10 TO 12 CUPS

⅔ cup unpeeled ground almonds (page 5)
½ cup sugar
1 tablespoon unbleached all-purpose flour
½ cup unsalted butter
2 tablespoons whole milk

Preheat the oven to 350°F.

In a medium saucepan or skillet, mix the almonds, sugar, and flour. Add the butter and milk, and cook over medium heat, stirring with a wooden spoon, until the butter is melted and all the ingredients are combined thoroughly.

Chill the batter in the freezer for 5 minutes. Make only 2 almond cups at a time; they spread while baking. Shape the batter into 1-inch rounds and place them 4 inches apart on a greased and floured baking sheet. Bake for 4 to 6 minutes until golden brown.

Allow only a few seconds to set, then remove the flat almond disks with a metal spatula and carefully place each one over the bottom of an inverted glass. Mold into a cup shape with your fingers. Let cool. Remove from the glass and turn each almond cup, right side up and place on a large tray until ready to fill. (Note: After removing the disks from the oven, if they harden too quickly, return them to the oven for 1 minute to soften and then shape them.) Repeat the process with the remaining batter.

PICCOLI SOUFFLÉS DI RICOTTA
(INDIVIDUAL RICOTTA SOUFFLÉS)

THIS CHEESECAKE-SOUFFLÉLIKE dessert makes a wonderful finale for a special dairy or fish dinner. I mix the cheese, egg yolks, and lemon zest several hours before the guests arrive. Then after dinner I fold the meringue into the egg-yolk mixture, fill the soufflé molds, and bake. No one minds waiting—especially when they taste these warm, light, and flavorful soufflés.

MAKES 8 SOUFFLÉS

2 tablespoons unsalted butter for molds

14 ounces fresh unsalted ricotta cheese

6 large eggs, separated

2 tablespoons grated lemon zest

1 tablespoon Sambuca or other anise-flavored liqueur

¾ cup granulated sugar

2 tablespoons confectioners' sugar

Preheat the oven to 350°F.

Brush eight 6-ounce soufflé molds with butter and place in the refrigerator.

In a large bowl, strain the ricotta (for a creamy consistency), by pressing it through a fine sieve or strainer. Add the egg yolks, one at a time, until well blended. Mix in the lemon zest and Sambuca. (At this point you can cover the mixture with plastic wrap and refrigerate up to 4 hours.)

In the large bowl of an electric mixer, beat the egg whites until foamy. Add ½ cup of the sugar and salt, and beat until stiff peaks form. Gently fold into the ricotta mixture.

Dust the prepared molds evenly with the remaining sugar. Line an ovenproof pan that is large enough to hold the cups with a cloth. Place the prepared molds in the pan and carefully spoon the ricotta mixture equally into the molds. Fill one third of the pan with hot water and bake for 20 minutes, or until soufflés are puffy and golden brown. Dust with confectioners' sugar and serve immediately.

SOUFFLÉS

Soufflés are delicate and require a cook's undivided attention. It's important to avoid opening the oven prematurely, which will cause the soufflés to fall. After 10 minutes' baking time, the soufflé will have risen above the top of the ramekin. The best way to tell if it is done is to touch the top gently to see if it is firm. Never use a toothpick to test doneness, as it will deflate the soufflé.

CELESTINO DRAGO'S TIRAMISÙ

TIRAMISÙ IS the quintessential Italian dessert, made with ultrarich Italian mascarpone cheese. There are many recipes for this famous dessert, but Celestino Drago, the talented chef-owner of Drago Ristorante in Santa Monica, California, serves the most delicious of all. And, as an extra bonus, it's easy to make.

MAKES 8 SERVINGS

> 6 large egg yolks
> 6 ounces sugar
> 2 teaspoons vanilla extract
> 8 ounces mascarpone or creamy ricotta cheese (see Note)
> 1 cup heavy cream
> 2 cups strong espresso coffee
> 36 ladyfingers
> Cocoa powder, for dusting

In a saucepan over very low heat, combine the egg yolks with 6 tablespoons water and cook for 3 minutes until mixture thickens like lemon curd and maintains a temperature of 160 degrees on a candy thermometer for at least 1 minute.

In a large bowl, mix the thickened egg yolks, sugar and vanilla. Beat until foamy. Add the mascarpone or creamy ricotta and beat until creamy and smooth.

In the bowl of an electric mixer, whip the cream until soft peaks form. Carefully fold the whipped cream into the egg yolk mixture. Cover with plastic wrap and refrigerate for 10 minutes.

Place the espresso in a shallow bowl and quickly dip the ladyfingers into it. Place the ladyfingers on a paper towel–lined baking sheet to absorb excess espresso.

Spread a layer of cream mixture on the bottom of an 8 × 10-inch glass baking dish. Top with a layer of ladyfingers, then cover with another layer of cream. Repeat the layers, ending with the cream mixture. Smooth with a wet spatula. Cover with plastic wrap and chill at least 1 hour before serving. Generously dust with cocoa powder.

NOTE: *Strain the ricotta cheese by pressing it through a fine sieve or strainer.*

STRAWBERRIES WITH RASPBERRY SAUCE

THIS SIMPLE dessert can turn an ordinary meal into an elegant one. It makes even pale strawberries look beautiful. To give its presentation pizzazz, serve it in a crystal or glass bowl and garnish with mint sprigs. Thin slices of pound cake go well with it, too.

MAKES 4 SERVINGS

2 pints fresh strawberries
1 pint fresh raspberries
One 8-ounce jar raspberry preserves
½–¾ cup sugar, depending on the sweetness of the fruit
⅓ cup kirsch or Concord grape wine

Trim the strawberries and raspberries and wash them in cold water. Drain on paper towels. Place the berries in a large bowl, cover with plastic wrap, and refrigerate.

In a food processor or blender, blend the preserves, sugar, and kirsch into a sauce. Press through a strainer to remove the seeds. Pour the sauce over the berries, cover with plastic wrap, and refrigerate for at least 20 minutes, and up to 1 hour, tossing from time to time, until you are ready to serve.

JOAN BRAM'S TRIPLE CHOCOLATE COOKIES

ONE DAY my friend Joan Bram, who often helps me test my recipes, brought me some of her intensely flavored chocolate cookies. They were so terrific, I asked her if I could put them in this book. So, here they are.

MAKES ABOUT 3 DOZEN COOKIES

2 tablespoons unsalted butter or nondairy margarine

6 ounces semisweet chocolate

2 ounces unsweetened chocolate

¼ cup sifted unbleached all-purpose flour

¼ teaspoon baking powder

⅛ teaspoon salt

2 large eggs

¾ cup sugar

2 teaspoons instant coffee

½ teaspoon vanilla extract

6 ounces semisweet chocolate chips

8 ounces toasted walnuts or pecans (page 101), broken into medium-sized pieces

Preheat the oven to 350°F.

In the top of a doubler boiler, over barely simmering water, melt the butter or margarine and chocolates, stirring constantly until smooth. Cool completely.

In a medium bowl, sift together the flour, baking powder, and salt. In the bowl of an electric mixer, beat together the eggs, sugar, instant coffee, and vanilla at high speed for 1 to 2 minutes, or until blended. On low speed, mix in cooled chocolate mixture and then sifted dry ingredients. Scrape bowl with a rubber spatula and beat only until blended. Stir in chocolate chips and walnuts.

Drop by heaping teaspoonfuls onto foil-lined baking sheets, 1 inch apart. Bake in the oven for 10 to 12 minutes on the top rack of the oven, or until dark brown and crisp around the edges.

PURIM SEED CRISPS

THIS RECIPE for the thinnest, most crisp cookies ever was adapted from one given to me by my friend Bernie Bubman. Bernie enjoys attending cooking classes in Europe, and he brought this recipe back from France. These crisps are a novel but delicious Purim dessert.

MAKE ABOUT 5 DOZEN COOKIES

5 tablespoons unsalted butter

5 tablespoons sugar

2 tablespoons Karo syrup

2 tablespoons whole milk

½ cup sesame seeds

2 tablespoons poppy seeds

2 tablespoons millet seeds (see Note)

Preheat the oven to 350°F.

In a medium skillet, over medium heat, cook the butter, sugar, Karo syrup, and milk, stirring with a wooden spoon, until the butter is melted and all the ingredients are combined thoroughly. Mix in the seeds. Transfer to a glass bowl. Refrigerate or freeze until firm, about 5 minutes.

Line a baking sheet with foil and shape the batter into 1-inch rounds the size of a nickel (the cookies spread a lot while baking). Place the rounds 2 inches apart on the prepared baking sheet. Bake for 10 minutes, or until golden brown. (Watch closely—they brown quickly.) Let cool and then carefully peel off the foil.

NOTE: *Millet seeds are available in most supermarkets and health food stores. The batter can be refrigerated for up to 3 days and stored in the freezer for 1 month.*

FRENCH TOAST "SANDWICH" SURPRISE

THE SURPRISE is a spoonful of berry preserves or warm melting chocolate inside each piece of French toast. If you like jelly doughnuts, you will love raspberry-filled French toast. Or if you like *pain au chocolat* (chocolate-filled croissants), this recipe also fills the bill.

Serve for breakfast or brunch with maple syrup or for dessert with a scoop of rich vanilla ice cream.

MAKES 8 SERVINGS

8 slices challah or white bread, about ½ inch thick
½ cup raspberry preserves, or 4 ounces semisweet chocolate, cut into ½-inch chunks
1 tablespoon water mixed with 1 tablespoon flour to make a paste
4 extra-large eggs
8 tablespoons milk
Unsalted butter, for frying
Confectioners' sugar, for garnish

Remove the crusts from the bread and discard; cut the bread into 16 triangles. Place 1 tablespoon preserves or a chunk of chocolate in the center of 8 of the triangles and brush the edges with the water-flour paste. Cover with the remaining 8 triangles, pressing the edges together firmly to seal.

In a medium shallow bowl, whisk together the eggs and milk. Dip each "sandwich" on both sides into the egg mixture just until moist.

In a large nonstick skillet, melt the butter over medium-high heat and sauté the "sandwiches" on both sides until golden brown. To serve, arrange each triangle on a heated serving plate and sprinkle with confectioners' sugar.

VARIATION: *Replace the preserves and chocolate with smoked salmon. Serve with sour cream or crème fraîche instead of maple syrup.*

QUEEN ESTHER'S TOAST

In Israel a bread fritter, moistened in milk and coated with beaten egg, is served during Purim; it's often called Queen Esther's Toast and is similar to what we know as French toast.

POTATO WAFFLE LATKES

MY FAMILY loves old-fashioned potato latkes, but they are always happy when I serve something new during Hanukkah. One year I surprised them with a low-fat potato waffle latke that was light, crisp, and delicious. It makes a super side dish for a dairy Hanukkah dinner or a novel dessert. I bake it in a nonstick Toastmaster waffle baker that has been lightly brushed with oil. The recipe will also work with an old-fashioned waffle iron. You can prepare the latkes in advance and, just before serving, heat them in a 350°F oven for 20 minutes, or until crisp.

MAKES 8 SERVINGS

3 large (about 2½ pounds) russet potatoes
¼ cup low-fat milk
1 tablespoon melted unsalted butter
1 teaspoon kosher salt
Pinch of ground white pepper
Vegetable oil, for brushing the waffle iron
Concord Grape Wine Syrup (recipe follows)

Peel the potatoes and cut into 2-inch cubes. Place them into a medium saucepan, cover with water, and bring to a boil over high heat. Reduce the heat and simmer until they are easily pierced with a fork, about 15 minutes. Drain well. Push the potatoes through a ricer or fine sieve. Measure 3 cups of the riced potatoes into a mixing bowl. Heat the milk and butter in a small saucepan or in a cup in the microwave oven, season with salt and pepper, then stir into the potatoes and mix well. Let cool. Divide the mixture into eight 3-ounce portions and shape each portion into a ball. (Note: For advance preparation, cover with plastic wrap and refrigerate until ready to use.)

Heat the waffle iron and brush with oil. Place one potato ball in the middle of the waffle griddle and close the lid by pressing gently. Bake for 4 to 5 minutes. Do not lift the lid until the waffle begins to steam, then carefully lift a corner of the waffle with the tines of a fork to loosen it and transfer it to a foil-lined baking sheet while the other waffles are baking.

Preheat the oven to 400°F. Heat the waffles in the oven until they become crisp again, about 10 minutes. Serve with Concord Grape Wine Syrup.

CONCORD GRAPE WINE SYRUP

1½ cups Concord grape wine or grape juice
½ cup sugar
1 tablespoon fresh grated orange zest

In a heavy medium saucepan, over medium-high heat, bring the wine and sugar to a boil, stirring frequently until the sugar dissolves. Stir in the zest and simmer until the sauce is reduced by one third, about 5 minutes. Serve hot or cold with waffles.

COCONUT SORBET

Inspired by a trip to Bali, this nondairy coconut sorbet has a texture as creamy as ice cream. Coconut milk is nondairy, and is sold in the Asian and Latin sections of most supermarkets.

MAKES 1 QUART

2 cups water
1½ cups sugar
4 cups coconut milk
2 tablespoons lime juice

In a large saucepan over high heat, bring the water and sugar to a boil. Remove from the heat and place over a bowl filled with ice water. Let cool. Stir in the coconut milk and lime juice; freeze in an ice cream maker according to the manufacturer's directions.

CHOCOLATE CHIP COCONUT SORBET

This cookbook would not be complete without including my technique for adapting the Coconut Sorbet recipe into make-believe chocolate chip ice cream.

Make Coconut Sorbet in an ice cream maker according to the manufacturer's instructions. When it is very cold and thick and while the machine is still running, pour warm melted chocolate in a thin stream into the mixture. The chocolate will quickly harden and break up into small pieces. Continue to freeze the sorbet. Spoon into plastic containers; cover and store in the freezer until ready to serve.

CHAPTER ELEVEN

✳

TAKE TIME
FOR
TRADITION

Although this book concentrates on time-saving recipes, I hope that all my readers are not always pressed for time, and that they enjoy observing the Sabbath and Jewish holidays with their family and friends.

The Jewish holidays and High Holy Days—and the Sabbath, too—are associated with special foods from our childhood. When we remember the Sabbath table, set with Mother's finest china, and the candles burning in her silver candlesticks, we also remember the smell of freshly baked challah, chicken soup with matzah balls, roast chicken, or well-seasoned brisket waiting in the oven. These memories stay with us forever, so share them with your family every chance you get.

Since I could not write a kosher cookbook without including some traditional favorites, I asked my family and recipe testers to name their favorite dishes. Here are the results.

THE JEWISH HOLIDAYS AND THEIR
SPECIAL FOODS

The Sabbath The most important holiday of the Jewish calendar, begins every Friday evening at sundown and lasts until nightfall on Saturday.

Classic Challah (page 175)
The Ultimate Chicken Soup with the Fluffiest Matzah Balls (page 178)
Cold Roasted Chicken with Fennel and Leeks (page 137)

Rosh Hashanah is the Jewish New Year. Festive family meals are an important part of this two-day holiday. Apples dipped in honey represent a "sweet year."

Braided Challah Rolls (page 177)
Cheese Kreplach (page 15)
Apple Pizza (page 154)

Yom Kippur is a day for fasting and prayer. A light family meal (prefast) is eaten prior to the holiday. The fast is broken after sunset the following day and then anything goes for the break-the-fast meal. Some families prefer a simple dairy menu, while others want to eat herring, smoked fish, and other deli buffet dishes.

Holiday Sweet Potato Kugel (page 180)
Kerstin's Swedish Potato and Gravlax Casserole (page 116)

Succot celebrates the fall harvest for one festive week. Meals are enjoyed outdoors in the *succah*, a little hut that re-creates the dwellings in which the ancient Jews lived during the harvest season.

Layered Salad (page 49)
Baked Stuffed Squash Blossoms (page 82)

Hanukkah is the Festival of Lights—an eight-day commemoration of the miracle of the one-day supply of oil that burned for eight days in the Temple in Jerusalem. The holiday is celebrated with parties and gift-giving. A variety of foods, many fried in oil, are traditionally served at Hanukkah meals.

Baked Sea Bass with Black Olive Sauce (page 119)
Potato Latkes with Chopped Olive Spread (page 70)
Potato Waffle Latkes (page 168)
Thomas Keller's Mashed Potato Latkes (page 23)

Purim is a happy holiday celebrating the rescue of Jews in ancient Persia. It's a fun day, with food and wine and children dressing up in costumes. And the celebration would certainly not be the same without hamantaschen.

Chicken Jambalaya (page 133)
Poppy Seed Hamantaschen (page 182)
Purim Seed Crisps (page 165)

Passover is an eight-day holiday that commemorates the exodus of the Jews from Egypt three thousand years ago. Matzah is, of course, the most significant component of the food served throughout the period, since no leavened bread can be eaten.

Gramma Gene's Gefilte Fish (page 183)
Passover Rosemary Rolls and Matzah Sticks (page 185)
Passover Hazelnut Sponge Cake (page 187)

Shavuot marks the spring harvest festival. The traditional foods for this holiday are dairy foods and those related to the harvest—grains, olives, honey, and figs.

Confetti Risotto (page 95)
Asparagus with Tomato Confit (page 83)

TAKE TIME FOR TRADITION

*

CLASSIC CHALLAH

BRAIDED CHALLAH ROLLS

THE ULTIMATE CHICKEN SOUP WITH THE FLUFFIEST MATZAH BALLS

COLD ROASTED CHICKEN WITH FENNEL AND LEEKS (PAGE 137)

HOLIDAY SWEET POTATO KUGEL

POPPY SEED HAMANTASCHEN

GRAMMA GENE'S GEFILTE FISH

PASSOVER ROSEMARY ROLLS AND MATZAH STICKS

PASSOVER HAZELNUT SPONGE CAKE

VEAL BREAST WITH TWO VEGETABLE STUFFINGS

AWARD-WINNING PERFECT POTATO LATKES

CLASSIC CHALLAH

BAKING CHALLAH is one of the oldest Shabbat traditions. Today, many young women are reviving this ritual. Here is my classic challah recipe. This European egg bread possesses a glossy brown crust and a moist, golden interior. Challah upgrades any sandwich and is the undisputed prime choice for making French toast.

MAKES 1 LARGE LOAF OR 2 SMALL LOAVES

1 package active dry yeast
1½ cups lukewarm water
Pinch of sugar
3 extra-large eggs
⅓ cup honey
4 tablespoons unsalted nondairy margarine, melted
1 tablespoon salt
5–6 cups unbleached all-purpose flour
Safflower oil or vegetable oil, for oiling dough, bowl, and baking sheet
Yellow cornmeal, for baking sheet
1 egg white, lightly beaten
Sesame seeds or poppy seeds, for garnish

In a glass measuring cup, sprinkle the yeast over ½ cup of the lukewarm water. Add the sugar, stir to dissolve, and set aside until foamy, about 2 minutes.

In the bowl of a heavy-duty electric mixer or a hand-held mixer, on low speed, beat together the 3 whole eggs, honey, and margarine. Add the remaining 1 cup lukewarm water and blend well. Blend in the yeast mixture. Add salt and 5 cups of the flour to the batter, 1 cup at a time, beating well after each addition, until the dough is thick enough to work by hand, about 2 minutes.

Turn out the dough onto a floured board and knead 5 minutes, adding enough additional flour to make a smooth and elastic dough. Place the dough in an oiled bowl; brush oil on top of the dough, cover with a towel, and let rise in a warm place until doubled in size, about 1 hour.

continued

Divide the dough into 3 portions, or 6 portions for 2 small loaves. Form each portion into a rope, about 8 inches long. Pinch together 1 end of each of the 3 ropes and braid the ropes, pinching the bottom ends together when you complete the braiding.

Lightly oil a baking sheet and generously sprinkle with cornmeal. Place the braided loaf on the sheet, cover with a towel, and let rise in a warm place until doubled in size, about 40 minutes. Meanwhile, preheat the oven to 350°F.

Brush the loaf with the egg white and sprinkle with sesame or poppy seeds. Bake about 30 to 40 minutes, or until golden brown and a hollow sound is made when tapped with a finger. Cool on a wire rack.

BRAIDED CHALLAH ROLLS

MAKES ABOUT 16 ROLLS

1 recipe Classic Challah dough (page 175)
Safflower oil or vegetable oil, for baking sheet
Yellow cornmeal, for baking sheet
1 large egg
3 tablespoons sesame or poppy seeds

Prepare the dough for Classic Challah.

Pull off a golf ball–sized piece of dough. Roll each piece into a 10 × 8 × 2-inch strip. Twist the dough strip into a rope, then tie the rope into a knot. Repeat with the remaining dough.

Lightly oil a baking sheet, sprinkle it with cornmeal, and place the rolls on it, about 2 inches apart. Cover and let rise in a warm place until doubled, about 45 minutes.

Preheat the oven to 350°F.

Lightly beat the egg and brush it over the rolls. Sprinkle the rolls with sesame or poppy seeds. Bake the rolls for about 30 minutes until golden brown. Transfer to wine racks to cool.

THE ULTIMATE CHICKEN SOUP WITH THE FLUFFIEST MATZAH BALLS

THIS CHICKEN soup really tastes like chicken. The secret is using lots of poultry and fresh vegetables, and simmering the soup until it's as rich as gravy. It can be frozen in ice-cube trays and added to sauces or other soups, or used to moisten leftover reheated chicken. If you don't have the time to make matzah balls, boil some noodles, macaroni, or ravioli and add them to the soup instead.

MAKES ABOUT 12 SERVINGS

One 5-pound chicken or two 3-pound chickens, trussed
1 pound chicken necks and gizzards, wrapped in cheesecloth and tied
3 medium yellow onions, peeled and diced
1 medium leek, sliced into 1-inch pieces
3–4 quarts water
16 small carrots, peeled and cut into 1-inch pieces
5 celery stalks with tops, cut into 1-inch pieces
3 medium parsnips, peeled and cut into 1-inch pieces
8 fresh parsley sprigs
Salt and freshly ground black pepper to taste
The Fluffiest Matzah Balls (recipe follows)

In a large, heavy Dutch oven or pot, place the chicken, cheesecloth containing the necks and gizzards, onions, leek, and enough water to cover. Over high heat, bring to a boil. Using a large spoon, skim off the scum that rises to the top. Add the carrots, celery, parsnips, and parsley. Cover, leaving the lid ajar, reduce the heat to low, and simmer for 1 hour. Season with salt and pepper. Uncover and simmer 30 minutes longer.

With a slotted spoon, remove the chicken and cheesecloth bundle from the soup. (Use the chicken for salad or bone and shred it and add it to the soup.) Let the soup cool to room temperature, then refrigerate it. Skim off the fat that hardens on the surface and discard it. Meanwhile, prepare the matzah balls.

Bring the soup to a boil and gently drop in the matzah balls. Cover, reduce the heat to low, and simmer for about 10 minutes (do not uncover during this cooking time). Ladle into heated soup bowls.

THE FLUFFIEST MATZAH BALLS

MY MOTHER made the lightest matzah balls I've ever tasted. However, I've perfected this recipe over the years, until now I am satisfied that mine are even lighter than hers.

MAKES ABOUT 12 MATZAH BALLS

3 eggs, separated
½–¾ cup cold water
1¼ cups matzah meal
⅛ teaspoon salt
Pinch of freshly ground black pepper
The Ultimate Chicken Soup (page 178)

Place the egg yolks in a measuring cup and add enough water to measure 1 cup. Beat the egg mixture with a fork until well blended. Set aside.

In a large bowl, using an electric mixer with the wire-whisk attachment, beat the egg whites until they form stiff peaks; do not overbeat. In a small bowl, combine the matzah meal, salt, and pepper. Using a rubber spatula, gently fold the yolk mixture alternately with the matzah meal mixture into the beaten egg whites. Season with salt and pepper. Dough will be sticky. Cover with a plate and let the dough firm up for 5 minutes.

Bring the chicken soup to a rolling boil over high heat. Spoon about ¼ cup dough into moistened palms and gently shape into rough balls. (Do not over-handle.) Drop into the boiling soup; do not crowd. When all the matzah balls are in the soup, cover, reduce the heat to low, and simmer for 10 minutes. (Do not lift the lid while the matzah balls are cooking.)

VARIATION: *To make Matzah Gnocchi, prepare the matzah dough according to the preceding recipe and spoon into a pastry bag with a ½-inch round tube opening. Bring a pot of water to a boil, then reduce the heat to a simmer. Hold the bag over the simmering water and squeeze out the dough in 1-inch lengths, cutting them off at the tip of the tube with a sharp knife. Cover and simmer for 10 minutes; do not uncover during this cooking time. Serve the gnocchi with your favorite pasta sauce.*

HOLIDAY SWEET POTATO KUGEL

A PLUMP, BEAUTIFULLY browned kugel adds a homey, old-fashioned accent to holiday menus. This one doesn't need a grain of sugar because the raisins and sweet potatoes provide natural sweetness. Another plus is that the top of this kugel forms a crisp crust. My little secret is to use a large baking dish, because the thinner the kugel, the crisper the crust.

MAKES 8 SERVINGS

Baked Sweet Potato (recipe follows)
12 ounces flat, wide egg noodles (about 7 cups)
8 cups lightly salted boiling water
½ cup unsalted nondairy margarine or vegetable oil
½ cup raisins, plumped in sweet wine or apple juice (see Note)
4 eggs, beaten
Salt and freshly ground black pepper to taste

Preheat the oven to 375°F.

Prepare the Baked Sweet Potato and set aside.

While the sweet potatoes are baking, cook the noodles in lightly salted boiling water until tender, 5 to 10 minutes. Place the noodles, margarine, Baked Sweet Potatoes, and drained plumped raisins in a large bowl. Add the eggs and season with salt and pepper. Mix well.

Spoon the mixture into a well-greased 9 × 13-inch baking dish. Bake for 35 to 45 minutes until the top is brown and crisp. Cut into squares. Serve hot or cold.

NOTE: *To plump raisins, soak them in sweet wine or apple juice for 1 hour, overnight, or 1 week. Squeeze dry and use when recipe calls for plumped raisins.*

BAKED SWEET POTATO

¼ cup extra-virgin olive oil
1 large (1 pound) sweet potato, peeled and cut into ½-inch dice (3½ cups)
Sugar to taste
Salt and freshly ground black pepper to taste

Preheat the oven to 400°F.

Lightly brush a 9 × 13-inch baking dish with olive oil. Toss the sweet potato in the olive oil and arrange in the baking dish in a single layer. Sprinkle with sugar and salt and pepper. Bake for 15 minutes, or until tender.

POPPY SEED HAMANTASCHEN

TWO **IMPORTANT** things to remember when preparing hamantaschen: The dough can be prepared in advance, wrapped in plastic wrap, then in foil or plastic bags, and stored in the refrigerator or freezer. The dough is then rolled out, filled, and baked just before serving. Second, the hamantaschen can be completely assembled, brushed with egg white, and stored in the refrigerator or freezer. Then defrost, bake, and serve them hot from the oven.

MAKES 5 TO 6 DOZEN

¼ pound unsalted butter or nondairy margarine, softened
½ cup sugar
3 eggs
Grated zest of 1 orange
2 cups unbleached all-purpose flour
1½ teaspoons baking powder
¼ teaspoon salt
1 tablespoon poppy seeds
Three 8-ounce cans poppy seed filling (see Note)

Preheat the oven to 375°F.

In the large bowl of an electric mixer, or with a hand mixer, blend the butter and sugar well. Beat in 2 eggs and the orange zest, mixing thoroughly. Add the flour, baking powder, salt, and poppy seeds; blend until the dough is smooth.

Transfer to a floured board and divide the dough into 3 or 4 portions for easier handling. Flatten each portion with the palm of your hand and roll it out ¼ inch thick. With a scalloped or plain cookie cutter, cut into 2½-inch rounds. Place 1 heaping teaspoon filling in the center of each round. Fold the edges of the dough toward the center to form a triangle, leaving a bit of the filling visible in the center. Pinch the edges to seal them.

Place the hamantaschen ½ inch apart on a lightly greased foil-lined baking sheet and brush with the remaining egg, lightly beaten. Bake for 10 minutes, or until golden brown. Transfer to wire racks to cool.

NOTE: *Poppy seed filling can be found in the dried fruit section or ethnic food section of most supermarkets.*

GRAMMA GENE'S GEFILTE FISH

THERE HAS always been a certain mystique surrounding the making of gefilte fish—did a precise recipe exist or not?

In our family, my mother-in-law was the maven, and one Passover she coached me in the art of making gefilte fish her way. The mystique included using an enormous selection of different fish, grinding and chopping them in a certain way with a special grinder and an oversized wooden chopping bowl. Now that she is gone, I am happy to have her recipe, which I have updated. Although now I use whole white fish and pike instead of an assortment, I still use a food grinder, never a food processor. And unless your fish vendor is a good friend, it's best to grind your own fish. That's part of the tradition.

This updated version of Gramma Gene's Gefilte Fish gets better every year.

MAKES ABOUT 50 FISH BALLS

Fish Broth (recipe follows)
7 pounds white fish and pike, filleted (bones, heads, and skin reserved) (see Note)
2 yellow onions, peeled and thinly sliced
4 carrots, peeled and thinly sliced
4 celery stalks, sliced
3 eggs
½ cup matzah meal
1 cup cold water
Kosher salt
Freshly ground black pepper
Fish roe (optional)
Lettuce, sliced cucumber, sliced beets, and horseradish sauce for garnish

Prepare the Fish Broth.

In a food grinder, grind the fish with the onions, carrots, and celery stalks. Put through the grinder again. Place the ground mixture in a large mixing bowl and blend with the eggs and matzah meal. Transfer the mixture to a large wooden chopping bowl and, using a hand chopper, chop the fish mixture, adding the water gradually with 1 tablespoon kosher salt and 2 teaspoons pepper as you chop. (Mixture should be soft and light to the touch.)

continued

Wet your hands with cold water and shape the fish mixture into oval balls. Bring the broth to a boil over high heat, and place the fish balls in the broth with the roe, if using. Cover, reduce the heat to medium high, and cook for 1 hour, or until fish is tender; do not overcook. Cool, transfer to a shallow glass bowl, cover with plastic wrap and foil, and refrigerate.

To serve, arrange a lettuce leaf on each plate; top with fish and garnish with cucumber and beets. Serve with horseradish sauce.

NOTE: *If possible, buy whole white fish. Have it boned and wrap the bones, heads, and skin separately. If you're lucky, you may find roe inside the fish, so you can poach it with the fish balls.*

FISH BROTH

MAKES ABOUT 1 QUART

3 yellow onions, coarsely diced (reserve peels)
2 carrots, peeled and thinly sliced
1 cup sliced celery tops
2 pounds fish bones, heads, and skin from filleted white fish
Salt and freshly ground black pepper to taste
Cold water

In a large pot, place the onions, onion peels, carrots, celery tops, fish bones, heads, and skin, and salt and pepper. Add water to cover and bring to a boil. Simmer for 1 hour, adding additional water if needed. Remove any scum that rises to the surface. When the broth is very flavorful, strain out the fish bones and vegetables and discard. Keep the broth warm.

PASSOVER ROSEMARY ROLLS AND MATZAH STICKS

BROWN-BAGGING TO school or the office during Passover doesn't mean taking only matzah sandwiches, which crumble all over the floor as well as your lap. When my children were school age, I always prepared Passover popover rolls for their lunch boxes. These updated sandwich rolls, flavored with onion and fresh rosemary, are fabulous to fill with leftover turkey, cranberry sauce, mayonnaise, and crispy lettuce, or to enclose chopped egg salad made out of the hard-boiled eggs from the seder dinner. Be sure to try the matzah stick variation, which is great to serve with a salad or main course during the remaining six days of Passover.

MAKES ABOUT 12 ROLLS

½ small yellow onion, peeled and diced

¼ cup fresh chopped rosemary, leaves only, stems removed, or 2 tablespoons dried
  rosemary

1 cup cold water

½ cup Passover safflower or vegetable oil

2 cups matzah meal

1 teaspoon salt

4 extra-large eggs

Preheat the oven to 375°F.

In a food processor or blender, place the onion and rosemary and blend. With the machine running, add ½ cup of the water in a thin stream and blend until it's almost a smooth puree with flecks of onion and rosemary. Transfer to a medium saucepan with the remaining ½ cup water and the oil and bring to a rolling boil over high heat.

In the large bowl of an electric mixer, or with a rubber spatula, combine the matzah meal and salt. Pour in the boiling water mixture and blend well. Add the eggs, one at a time, beating well after each addition until completely blended. Cover and let rest for 10 minutes.

continued

With well-oiled hands, shape the dough into 2- or 3-inch balls or ovals and place 2 inches apart on a well-greased foil-lined baking sheet. Bake for 40 to 50 minutes, or until golden brown. Transfer to wire racks and cool.

FOR MATZAH STICKS: *Sprinkle matzah meal or matzah cake meal on the work surface. Shape about ¼ cup of the dough into an oval and roll, in a back-and-forth motion, until it measures about 12 inches long by 1 inch round to resemble a breadstick. Repeat with the remaining dough. Place each matzah stick, 1 inch apart, on a well-greased foil-lined baking sheet, brush with oil, and sprinkle with kosher salt. Bake in a preheated 375°F oven for 25 minutes, or until golden brown and crispy. Makes about 14 matzah sticks.*

PASSOVER HAZELNUT SPONGE CAKE

A DELICIOUS CHANGE from old-fashioned Passover sponge cakes, this is a flavorful blend of orange, hazelnuts, and chocolate that rises to lovely new heights.

MAKES ABOUT 12 SERVINGS

7 eggs, separated
1⅓ cups sugar
½ cup orange juice
2 tablespoons grated orange zest
½ cup matzah cake meal
½ cup potato starch (see Note)
¾ cup ground hazelnuts, toasted (page 101)
3 tablespoons chopped semisweet chocolate
Pinch of salt
Chocolate Glaze or Sauce (page 158)

Preheat the oven to 325°F.

In the large bowl of an electric mixer, or with a hand mixer, beat the egg yolks and 1 cup of the sugar until light in color and texture. Add the orange juice and grated orange zest and blend well. Gradually blend in the matzah cake meal, potato starch, hazelnuts, and chocolate.

Beat the egg whites and salt until foamy and gradually add remaining sugar, 1 tablespoon at a time, beating until stiff enough to hold a peak. Gently fold them into the yolk mixture.

Pour the batter into an ungreased 10-inch tube pan. Bake for 1 hour, or until the cake springs back to the touch and a toothpick inserted in the cake comes out dry. Remove the cake from the oven; immediately invert the pan and let it cool. Loosen the sides and center of the cake with a sharp knife and unmold it onto a cake plate. Garnish with Chocolate Glaze.

NOTE: *Potato starch can be found in most supermarkets in the kosher food department or kosher markets.*

VEAL BREAST WITH
TWO VEGETABLE STUFFINGS

MY **MOTHER'S** vegetable stuffings are European in origin, and were inherited from her mother-in-law, my paternal grandmother. The large amount of fresh vegetables used in both make them entirely different from ordinary starchy stuffings.

Use the stuffing with oatmeal to fill a veal breast, turkey, or chicken for Shabbat; and the recipe using matzah meal for Passover dishes. And if there is any unbaked stuffing left over, bake it in a casserole.

MAKES 8 SERVINGS

Molly's Vegetable Stuffing (page 189)
Passover Vegetable Stuffing (page 190)
One 6- to 8-pound veal breast, trimmed of fat, with pocket for stuffing
Salt and freshly ground black pepper to taste
4 tablespoons extra-virgin olive oil
2 onions, peeled and thinly sliced
3 garlic cloves, minced
4 carrots, peeled and thinly sliced
1 parsnip, peeled and thinly sliced
2 celery stalks, thinly sliced
1 bay leaf, crushed
½ cup minced fresh parsley
One 10 ½-ounce can tomato sauce
1 cup dry red wine

Preheat the oven to 375°F.

Prepare Molly's Vegetable Stuffing or the Passover Vegetable Stuffing.

Season the veal with salt and pepper. Stuff the pocket of the veal with stuffing and close the pocket with a needle and white thread. Remove the thread before serving.

In a large roasting pot, heat the olive oil and sauté the onions and garlic until soft, about 5 minutes. Add the carrots, parsnip, celery, bay leaf, parsley, tomato sauce, and wine and bring to a simmer. Add the veal breast and baste with the sauce. Cover and bake for 2 hours, basting every 20 minutes, until tender. Bake uncovered the last 30 minutes.

MOLLY'S VEGETABLE STUFFING

MAKES ABOUT 12 CUPS

¼ cup extra-virgin olive oil

3 medium onions, peeled and finely chopped

3 garlic cloves, minced

4 celery stalks, finely diced

6 medium carrots, peeled and grated

1 parsnip, peeled and grated

2 medium zucchini, unpeeled and grated

½ cup raisins, plumped in 1 cup Concord grape wine (see Note, page 180)

½ cup minced fresh parsley

2–3 tablespoons oatmeal

2–3 tablespoons unbleached all-purpose flour

2–3 tablespoons dry bread crumbs

¼ cup dry red wine

Salt and freshly ground black pepper to taste

In a large, heavy skillet, heat the oil and sauté the onions and garlic until soft, about 3 minutes. Add the celery, carrots, parsnip, and zucchini, and toss well. Cook for 5 minutes until the vegetables begin to soften. Drain the raisins and add them to the vegetables with the parsley. Stir in 1 tablespoon each of the oatmeal, flour, and bread crumbs. Add the wine and mix well. Stir in the remaining dry ingredients, a little at a time, until the stuffing is moist and soft but firm in texture. Season with salt and pepper. Cool.

PASSOVER VEGETABLE STUFFING

IADAPTED MY mother's vegetable stuffing for Passover, substituting matzah meal, matzah cake meal, and potato starch. It has become a family heirloom treasured for the happy memories it evokes of family celebrations. While my mother's recipe dates back to a time before food processors, I chop the onions, garlic, and celery in the food processor fitted with the knife blade. Then I change to the grater blade and grate the carrots, parsnip, and zucchini, and what took her hours to make takes me about 5 minutes.

MAKES ABOUT 12 CUPS

¼ cup extra-virgin olive oil

3 medium onions, peeled and finely chopped

3 garlic cloves, minced

4 stalks celery, finely diced

6 medium carrots, peeled and grated

1 parsnip, peeled and grated

2 medium zucchini, unpeeled and grated

½ cup raisins, plumped in 1 cup Concord grape wine (see Note, page 180)

½ cup minced fresh parsley

2–3 tablespoons matzah meal

2–3 tablespoons matzah cake meal

2–3 tablespoons Passover potato starch or Passover cereal (see Note)

¼ cup dry red wine

Salt and freshly ground black pepper to taste

In a large, heavy skillet, heat the oil and sauté the onions and garlic until soft, about 3 minutes. Add the celery, carrots, parsnip, and zucchini, and toss well. Cook for 5 minutes until the vegetables begin to soften. Drain the raisins and add them to the vegetables with the parsley. Stir in 1 tablespoon each of the matzah meal, matzah cake meal, and potato starch. Add the wine and mix well. Stir in the remaining dry ingredients, a little at a time, until the stuffing is moist and soft but firm in texture. Season with salt and pepper. Cool.

NOTE: *Potato starch and Passover cereal can be found in most supermarkets in the kosher food department or kosher markets.*

AWARD-WINNING PERFECT POTATO LATKES

THIS LATKE recipe was chosen as one of the top 10 recipes of 1998 by the *Los Angeles Times.* "The best we've ever eaten," said its test kitchen and food editors.

MAKES 1 DOZEN LATKES, OR 4 SERVINGS

4 baking potatoes, peeled
1 large yellow onion, peeled and grated
1 tablespoon fresh lemon juice
4 extra-large eggs
3 tablespoons unbleached all-purpose flour
Pinch of baking soda
1 teaspoon salt
Freshly ground black pepper to taste
Vegetable oil, for frying

Grate the potatoes, using a food processor or fine shredder. Immediately transfer the potatoes to a large bowl and add the onion, lemon juice, eggs, flour, baking soda, and salt and pepper. Mix well.

Heat ⅛ inch of oil in a nonstick skillet over medium heat. Pour the batter into the hot oil with a large spoon and flatten with the back of the spoon to make 4-inch latkes. Cook on one side until golden brown, 3 to 5 minutes; then turn and cook on the other side, about 2 minutes. (Turn once only.) Drain well on paper towels and serve immediately, plain or with topping.

INDEX